D1715367

HISTORY OF ASIA

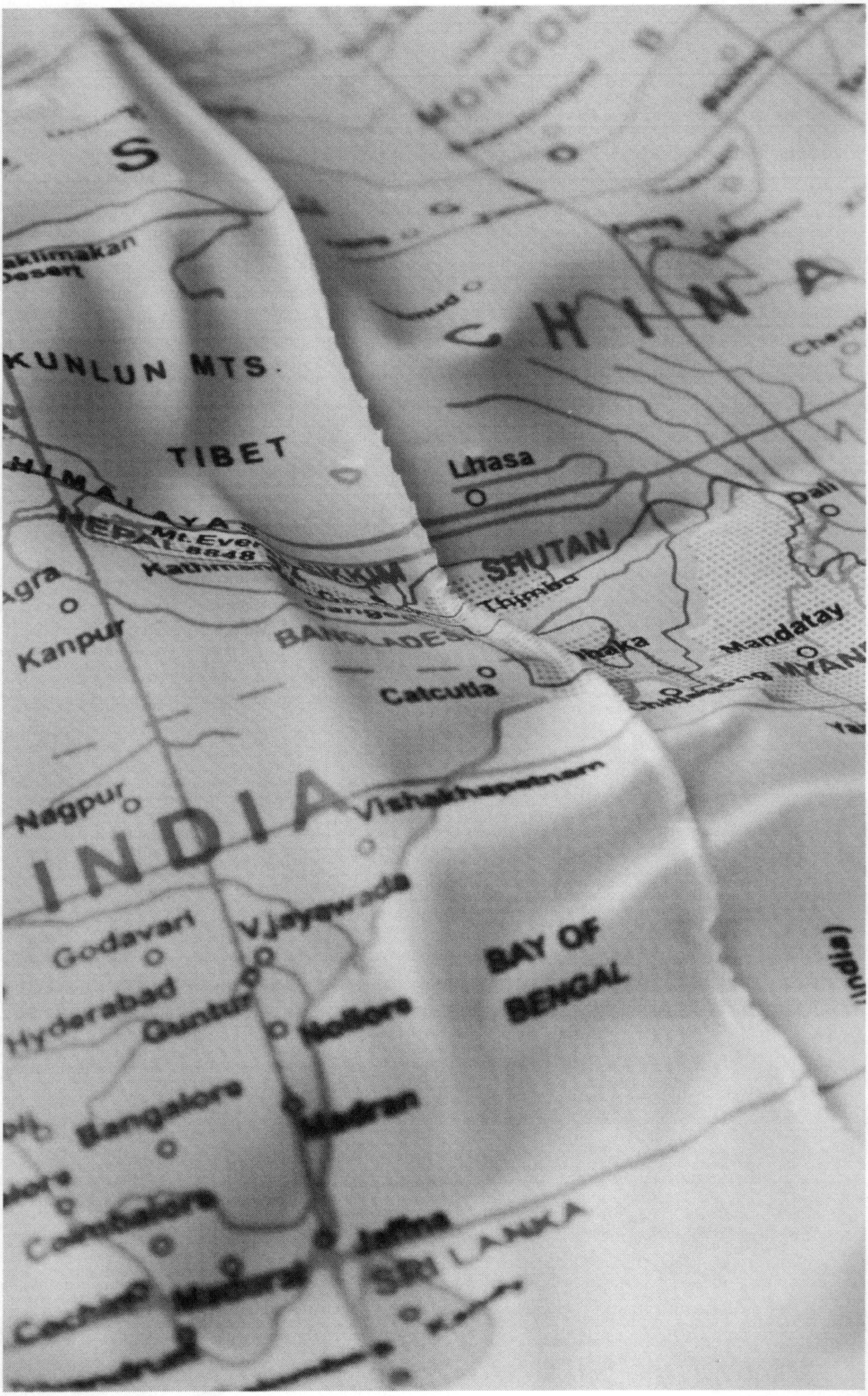

KUNLUN MTS.
TIBET
CHINA
Lhasa
HIMALAYAS
NEPAL
Agra
Kanpur
Calcutta
Dali
Mandalay
BAY OF
BENGAL
INDIA
Nagpur
Godavari
Hyderabad
Bangalore
SRI LANKA

HISTORY OF ASIA

Published 2023 by History Brought Alive

FREE BONUS FROM HBA: EBOOK BUNDLE

Greetings!

First of all, thank you for reading our books. As fellow passionate readers of History and Mythology, we aim to create the very best books for our readers.

Now, we invite you to join our VIP list. As a welcome gift, we offer the History & Mythology Ebook Bundle below for free. Plus you can be the first to receive new books and exclusives! Remember it's 100% free to join.

Simply scan the QR code down below to join.

CONTENTS

THE HISTORY OF CHINA

JAPANESE HISTORY

THE HISTORY OF INDIA

THE HISTORY OF CHINA

INTRODUCTION

China is one of the world's great civilizations. Unlike other comparable civilizations of bygone eras, such as those in ancient Egypt, Mesopotamia, or the Indus Valley, China's civilization is not only ancient but continuous. Whereas the monuments of other great civilizations now lie in ruins; their people scattered or colonized by newcomers, and their languages dead or forgotten; the language, culture, and people of China have endured, persisting through the millennia until this very day. For this reason, **China represents the world's oldest living civilization**.

Astonishingly, for over 2000 of the past 5000 years of recorded human history, the achievements of Chinese civilization are beyond compared. In that time, China led the world in astronomy, chemistry, medicine, agriculture, metallurgy, the arts, and the art of war. It had the biggest population, the wealthiest treasury, the greatest fleets, the most advanced technology, the strongest military, and the largest effectively planned cities. China was not only at the center of world trade, but it was also the center of tribute for foreign nations who could not hope to compare with its power.

Despite this rarified status in world history, public knowledge of history of China is sorely lacking. Many people in western cultures can name more than one Roman Emperor, but how many can name a Chinese Emperor? We argue that the Emperors of China are of equal significance. It is for this reason that History Brought Alive brings you this concise, comprehensive, and accurate history of China.

You may have already tried to learn about Chinese history and have found it to be an unpleasant task. Most currently available books on the topic are unwieldy, written in lengthy and dense academic prose. Few cover the entire sweep of Chinese history in chronological order, and, due to China's position as the last remaining communist-governed world power, some authors present a bias towards or against its political ideology. Should learning about this awe-inspiring civilization be uncomfortable and uninteresting? Absolutely not—this is the book for you!

Together, we will journey through Chinese history in an immersive and engaging manner, while revealing its fascinating humanity and epic grandeur. Beginning from the earliest creation myths and the first archeological evidence of complex societies, we will ground your understanding in the foundations of China's past. The all-important geographical context of these fledgling societies will then be discussed. Once the reader is familiar with the Yellow River Basin and these deep roots of Chinese culture, we will progress sequentially through the five eras of Chinese history: Ancient China, the First Imperial Age, the Second Imperial Age, the Third Imperial Age, and the Modern Age.

At each step of the journey, we will be confronted by the trials and tribulations faced by the Chinese people. These may be external challenges, such as foreign invaders or rival nations, or internal challenges, such as natural disasters or social rebellions. The remarkable responses of the Chinese people in the face of these difficulties will be discussed innovations in governance, education, agriculture, technology, and military organization. A cast of exceptional characters will be introduced as we move through time—some heroic, some villainous, some tragic—enabling us to personally identify with the highs and lows experienced by this epic civilization.

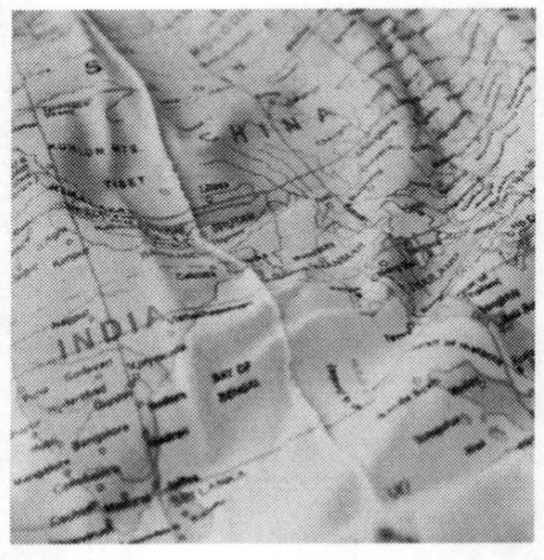

As you read, you will discover a social philosophy that has spread across East Asia, and a unique indigenous religion practiced by millions. You will be confronted by great leaders and their incredible military campaigns. World firsts, including inventions important to global histories, such as paper money, insurance, and the moveable-type printing press, will be introduced. The shattering effect of 20th-century history and China's place in World War II will be explored in-depth, and we will end with a discussion of the rise of the contemporary People's Republic of China.

By the conclusion of the journey, the reader will be well-versed with Chinese culture and the unique circumstances and character of its people. The concise nature of the book is expanded upon by a list of authoritative references for those who wish to dive deeper into over 6000 years of drama and intrigue. Written without political bias, this book will enable you to interact more effectively with people from China—a most important goal in this globalized age.

We at **History Brought Alive** pride ourselves on

producing expertly crafted works that enrich the reader and provide new insights into the past. Our existing titles include books on Roman history, Greek mythology, Norse mythology, Ancient Egyptian history, among many more. Well-written, thoroughly researched, and comprehensive, this history of China is yet another must-have on your shelf from **History Brought Alive**.

China in 2021 represents the world's second-largest economy and the world's biggest manufacturer. In today's globalized world, we are all linked in some way to China. If you wear clothes from brands like Adidas or Prada, if you own electronics made by giants such as Apple or Dell, or if you drive a Volkswagen or a Honda, you are in a trading relationship with China. Professionally, you may have Chinese colleagues or interact with Chinese clients. Your company may even be Chinese owned! This book is therefore indispensable, not only for students of history but for all of us making our way in the contemporary world.

Learning about China in the 21st century is critically important. Read on, to discover the remarkable history of China. This book presents an immersive, engaging, and exciting journey into China's past—a story of vast geographic scope, encompassing over ten thousand years of archeological history and involving the lives of billions of people.

This is how history should be told: **History Brought Alive**.

CHAPTER 1

A TIME OF MYTH AND LEGEND

How did the world begin? Every culture and civilization have its own legends. The Chinese creation myth, unlike those of western cultures, begins not with a first cause, but with a Great Void:

In the beginning, there was nothing. No time, no space, no phenomena, no appearance. Only a cosmic void pregnant with potential. Within the potential of this void, an egg grew. Within the egg there appeared the positive force of yang and the negative force of yin. A hairy, horned giant, the first being, grew within this egg. His name was Pangu. With a roar, he cleaved the forces of yin and yang apart and broke the cosmic egg.

Pangu pushed yang upwards to become the sky and trod yin beneath him so that it became the earth. He grew in size and might, separating earth and sky far apart until eventually his work was done. Satisfied, he died. As he died, his body transformed. His blood became the rivers; his sweat the rain; his breath the wind; and his voice, thunder. Pangu's limbs became the earth and his torso the mountains, his hair, and beard the stars and planets. The moon was his right eye, and his left eye, the sun. The world was formed from Pangu (Keay, 2009).

Millions of years passed, and many divine beings emerged within the world. Fuxi and Nuwa were twin beings, both brother-sister, and husband-wife. Nuwa sculpted figures from the yellow clay of the great river and gave them life—these living clay figures were the first human beings. Fuxi tamed animals, studied the heavens, and through his marriage to Nuwa, instituted the family.

The next great being who emerged was Shennong. Shennong gave humanity the gift of agriculture, the knowledge of digging wells, and the practice of herbal medicine. His successor was known as the Yellow Emperor. The Yellow Emperor taught humanity the use of weaponry and led the tribes of the Yellow River to victory in their first-ever battle; the battle of Banquan.

These divine culture heroes created the basis of Chinese civilization—a feudal military civilization with knowledge of agriculture and medicine, based on the institution of the family. On the banks of the Yellow River, this civilization prospered and grew until disaster struck. The river itself, the giver of life, became the enemy, flooding uncontrollably and destroying everything in its path.

It was at this time that a new hero emerged; the Yellow Emperor's great-great-grandson: Yu. Yu rebelled against the water-control management practices of the time—instead of damming rivers, he dredged them; instead of reinforcing riverbanks, he dug overflow channels to carry excess water into the fields. His approach was an incredible success, and the raging river was tamed. Indebted, the King of the time offered him the throne, and Yu the Great became the founder of the Xia Dynasty (Wright, 2011).

Geography

These are China's foundational myths and legends, but what about the objective truth? The story of China begins with the stories of two things: the story of a people, the ethnic Han, and the story of a river, the Huang Ho, or the Yellow River.

The Yellow River rises high in the Tibetan Plateau, over four thousand meters above sea level, and over five thousand kilometers from the sea. In its upper course, it runs swift and crystal clear across the high plateau, before plunging through a series of gorges and cataracts. Down it falls until it spreads onto the Loess Plateau. Here the river turns north, then east, then south, tracing a great loop across north-central China. Particulate matter blown in from the deserts and steppes to the north and west compose the loess plateau; in places, this sediment is tens to hundreds of meters thick. The river erodes this fertile soil, becoming heavy with the yellow silt that provides it with its name. On completion of its great loop, the river turns east, spreading out across the north China plain on its way to the sea. Here the river brings the gift and curse of the Loess—the fertility and the sedimentation of the silt. As the silt settles on the riverbed, it gradually raises the river to the level of the surrounding land. When spring floods come, the river is liable to burst its banks, or even change course completely, wreaking death and destruction across the land (Wright, 2011).

Archeology

Modern visitors to China may be surprised to find that it is a country of 56 official ethnic groups and 302 recognized languages. In ancient times China was even more ethnically and culturally diverse. But the story of China is, to a large extent, the story of the prosperity and rise to dominance of a people known as the ethnic Han. The ethnic Han makes up the majority of the 1.4 billion population of contemporary China, and the majority of the 50 million people of the modern Chinese diaspora. Genetic evidence ties the modern Han Chinese population to the peoples of the Yellow River who lived three thousand years ago (Zhao et al, 2015).

Archeological evidence reveals that the lives of the hunter-gatherer tribes who lived by the Yellow River began to transform around 8000 BCE with the domestication of the cereal crop millet. Four thousand years later, wet rice cropping was introduced from the south, enabling plentiful harvests. The secret of silk soon followed—a secret the Chinese were to the harbor for millennia—and then metallurgy developed. By 2700 BCE, the tribes of the Yellow River knew how to work jade and many of the basic elements of what we now know as Chinese culture were in place.

Remarkably, the fanciful legends of divine beings parallel the development of Chinese civilization. Fuxi and Nuwa could be thought of as representing the tribal era; Shennong, the agricultural; and the Yellow Emperor an organized military state possessing the ability to work metals and jade (Ferguson & Masaharu, 1928). But what of Yu the Great and his mastery of the waters? Incredibly, there is archeological evidence of a period of catastrophic flooding of the Yellow River beginning 1920 BCE, with a renewal of cultural development following in its wake (Wu et al, 2016).

The First Kingdoms

The culture arising in the wake of the great flood of 1920 BCE may have been the Xia dynasty, however, without written evidence, archeologists are reluctant to apply a definitive label. The first dynasty of China according to written evidence is the Shang dynasty, which was founded in 1600 BCE. We know of the Shang dynasty because their earliest writing, taking the form of pictographs scratched into bone, is the direct predecessor of the modern Chinese script (Wright, 2011). The artful, stylized calligraphy that we recognize as the written Chinese of today is a descendant of the Shang practice of drawing pictures to represent things and ideas.

Shang society was one of the aristocrats served by shaman-priests, who ruled over commoners and slaves. Two of the classic features of Chinese religious life were already in place at this time: the worship of ancestors, and the practice of divination (the earliest writing was found on burnt bones that had been used as oracles) (Cao & Sun, 2011). Bronze working was refined to a high level of sophistication, and bronze ware decorated palaces and equipped their formidable military.

The Shang dynasty lasted for an astonishing 600 years. Later writings, which cannot be regarded as a reliable, state

that the late Kings of the dynasty became tyrannical. An aristocratic rebellion led to a civil war which was won by a man named Fa Ji, who became King Wu, founder of the Zhou Dynasty. His brother, known as the Duke of Wu, assisted in strengthening and consolidating the newly won kingdom. As the Shang were a society that practiced divination and so claimed to be a kingship guided by the divine, the Duke of Wu introduced a counterclaim to legitimize the new dynasty. The Duke explained that the **Mandate of Heaven**, the will of the divine, existed to ensure a just ruler. If the rulers were unjust, as the Shang were believed to be, then Heaven would see to it that a new, better, and more just, the dynasty would arise to take their place (Kerr, 2013).

The Spring and Autumn Period

The Zhou kingship continued in slow decline for three hundred years, as the power of its feudal vassals grew. Eventually, in 771 BCE, one of the vassals, the Marquess of Shen, allied with nomadic tribes and sacked the capital. King You of Zhou was killed, and the court fled east from their heartland on the Wei River, establishing a new capital city downstream on the lower Yellow River.

So begins the timeline of what is known as the Eastern Zhou Dynasty. A classic of Chinese literature written during this period, *The Spring and Autumn Annals*, gives its name to the first three hundred years of the Eastern Zhou. The Zhou system was a network of production and distribution controlled by feudal landowners, with their vassalage centralized around the king. Commoners were obligated to complete work in their feudal master's fields before time was allotted to tend their personal plots. The produce of these feudal fields was presented as a tribute to the King, who in turn rationed it to the populace as necessary. The practice of gift-giving circulated luxuries amongst the upper classes.

With the move of the Zhou court eastward, this system began to break down. New iron tools and ox-driven plowing techniques vastly improved the efficiency of agricultural labor. Workers began to resent the time spent on forced labor, and landowners were driven to lease out the communal land in exchange for rent that they kept, rather than presented to the King. This process of the privatization of land and property accelerated, in turn driving demand for the products of artisans and stimulating long-distance trade. By the end of the Spring and Autumn period, coins were being minted and a vibrant market economy had taken root. In this time of incredible change, some feudal lords became destitute while others prospered, and the common person was enabled to develop and financially benefit from his or her individual talents (Zhang, 2015).

A Flowering of Philosophy

The development of the market economy was able to support a new class of individuals. These were the scholars, who, thanks to long-distance trading, could now move more freely across the land, and no longer restricted by clan boundaries, they were able to discuss and exchange ideas. This was the beginning of the *"one hundred schools of thought"*—the incipient intellectual sphere of the Chinese cultural world. Two of these schools would go on to become major pillars in the foundations of Chinese culture; the Confucians, and the Daoists.

The Daoists

The major text of the Daoists, the Dao de Jing, was written by Laozi. In legend, he was considered to be a royal record keeper in the court of the Eastern Zhou. Long-lived and wise,

he eventually tired of the corruption of civic and royal life and retreated from society into the mountains. Before he left forever, he compiled his teaching into the Dao de Jing.

In this work, he describes the birth of the Cosmos and outlines the path of living a life in harmony with the workings of the Cosmos, which he named the Dao or the Way. His teaching, known as Daoism, was to become the predominant indigenous religion of China, and its philosophy informed the entirety of Chinese thought that followed (Cao & Sun, 2011).

The Confucians

Confucius (also known as Kongzi), whose existence has much more historical veracity than that of Laozi, was considered as a younger contemporary of the latter. Whereas Laozi counseled a retreat from society and a return to nature, Confucius was concerned with the problem of how to live an effective life within society. He created the idea of a moral society based on benevolent goodwill to all people and deference to authority. In Confucianism, the ideal of the moral man, who knew his place within the social order, and who strived for perfection through self-cultivation was established. The records of his teachings, *The Analects*, would go on to provide not only the ethical foundation of Chinese culture, but also the ethical foundation of Japanese, Korean, and Vietnamese society (Wright, 2011).

This "Spring and Autumn" era of the Eastern Zhou lasted from 771 BCE to 476 BCE. During this time, the influence of the Eastern Zhou kings steadily waned as their feudal vassals expanded their territory and exerted their autonomy.

Gradually, the hundreds of petty fiefdoms supposedly subservient to the Zhou king consolidated, either through warfare or by the alliance. With the partition of the state of Jin in 453 BCE, only seven states remained, and the stage was set for conflict. Which of the seven states would be able to reign supreme?

永乐皇帝朱棣

CHAPTER 2
THE FIRST EMPEROR

March 1974. Six brothers were digging a well in a field near the city of Xian. They dug steadily downward; down through the changing shades of different layers of earth, until, with a *clang*, their spades hit something hard. One of the brothers pulled up the obstruction—it was a piece of terracotta.

How strange, they thought.

As they worked, they scooped up more and more fragments of terracotta, bricks made of terracotta, and small pieces of bronze. Little did they know that they had discovered bronze arrowheads, the brick foundations of an enclosure, and pieces of an army of life-sized terracotta warriors—an army built to guard the resting place of the First Emperor of China (Wright, 2011).

The Warring States

Yan, Qi, Wei, Chu, Zhou, Han, and Qin were the names of the seven states that occupied the heartland of China at the tail end of the Eastern Zhou dynasty; a heartland that had grown from its historic center on the eastwards bend of the Yellow River to also encapsulate the lower reaches of the second great river of China, the Chiang Jiang (known to the west as the

Yangtze). These two mighty rivers, and their surrounding floodplains and highlands, would be the field where the battle for control of China would play out.

At the outset of hostilities, Qin was one of the smaller states vying for domination, and in the early years of the period, it played a marginal role in the wars and intrigues of the time. Qin's placement of the western margins of Chinese civilization, however, gave it a geographical advantage: the state's location on the banks of the Wei River meant that it was protected by mountains to its north, south, and west. It only had to worry about the invasion from the east.

The Qin leadership made wise use of their circumstances. In 361 BCE, they appointed Shang Yang, a luminary of one of the thousand schools of thought, to the position of the chief minister. Shang Yan was not a Confucian or a Daoist, he was a Legalist, who believed in absolute law enforced by absolute power. His vision was of a society centralized under an absolute ruler, and he believed that the purpose of every individual person was to work tirelessly in support of this society. Shan Yang used his new office to put his theory into practice, reducing the power of the Qin aristocracy and centralizing the military under the King of Qin. Forced labor became the task of the common people, with only the most productive able to take on other roles. The State of Qin was honed into a singular instrument of war (Zhang, 2011).

Qin Shi Huang Di

Thanks to Shang Yang's influence, the power of the Qin state steadily grew. Qin annexed the plains of the Sichuan Basin to the southwest, and, through a revolutionary system of irrigation and flood control, increased their fertility. The other states of China recognized Qin's rising menace and sought to check its power. Some court intellectuals, drawn from the ranks of the one hundred schools of thought, counseled a “vertical alliance” whereby Yan, Qi, Wei, Chou, Zhou, and Han would join forces to make a power block that was capable of resisting or even defeating the Qin. An alternative school of thought was the “horizontal alliance,” which promoted the idea of a state allying itself to Qin in order to break this deadlock. This state would then support Qin’s rise to dominance as a partner in power.

In the year 247 BCE, a new king inherited the throne of Qin. Ying Zheng, only 13-years-old at the time of his ascension, would go on to distinguish himself as a remarkable leader and a cunning tactician. By 235 BCE, he had rid the Qin court of all rivals and, by 230 BCE, he had formulated a strategy to conquer all of China; he would ally with the states most distant from Qin, and attack the states nearest to Qin. In this way, he would encourage the ambitions of those states wishing to form a “horizontal alliance” and undermine the threat of any “vertical alliance” against him.

The bordering kingdom of Han was the first state to fall. Qin then took advantage of natural disasters to invade Zhou. Wei was conquered after whole rivers were diverted to flood its capital. Chu was next to be vanquished, followed by Yan. Qi, the last remaining state and “ally” to Qin, surrendered in order to save its people from the massacre. Ying Zheng had conquered all of the lands of the former Zhou dynasty, and he bestowed upon himself a new title: “Qin Shi Huang Di”. Echoing the legend of “Huang Di” or the Yellow Emperor, he had named himself *The First Emperor of the Qin Dynasty* (Cao & Sun, 2011).

The Qin Empire

Qin Shi Huang Di's military campaigns did not cease with the defeat of the Qi state. He sent his generals south, where they conquered the regions of southern China that were not ethnically Han, and to the northeast, where they defeated the nomadic tribes that had, for millennia, menaced the frontiers of Chinese civilization. To prevent the re-incursion of the nomads, the Emperor ordered the building of a rammed earth barrier across the northern frontier; this would form part of the foundation of the later Great Wall of China.

The new Emperor now turned his attention to statecraft, and together with his brilliant minister Li Si, another Legalist in the tradition of Shang Yang, Qin Shi Huang Di set about transforming China into a singular state under his supreme rule. The feudal system that had, for centuries, provided the structure of Chinese civilization was abolished in a single stroke. The state became the sole owner of the land, and a system of civil administration was created to administer public works and to manage taxation. This hierarchical structure, unlike the hereditary land ownership that preceded it, was appointed through ability and merit. Chinese script was standardized, as were the weights and measures used at markets, and a new currency was minted.

Great public works were enacted, including new roads and canals, and a countrywide census informed the leadership of every detail of the land and people. Political thought was strictly controlled, and in a famous incident over which Li Si presided, the Confucian classics were burned and the scholars who did not denounce these works were buried alive. Within a generation, the Warring States had been transformed into a singular Empire. When Qin Shi Huang Di died in his eleventh year of rule, he was buried in a mausoleum the size of a city. Eternally guarded by an army of life-sized terracotta soldiers that would watch over his grave remained undisturbed, and unrecorded by history, until that fateful digging of a well in the spring of 1974 (Wright, 2011).

The Han Empire

Qin Shi Huang Di's new empire did not last long. His heirs became puppets of court intrigue, and the harsh punishments of the Empire's Legalist regime began to antagonize the populace. A two-faction rebellion broke out, with both led by army deserters, and, after five years of war, the Qin Empire was overthrown.

Emperor Gaozu of the Han dynasty took his seat of authority. Emperor Gaozu threw himself into the task of revitalizing the Empire. To the generals that had accompanied him to victory, he gifted kingdoms, partially recreating the feudal system, but he also maintained Qin Shi Huang Di's merit-based system of officialdom. The tax burden on the populace was reduced, and the growth of families was encouraged by exempting new parents from forced labor. Agricultural production was prioritized.

Gaozu's example of the rule in service to the people was followed by his successors, and by the time of the fifth Emperor of the Han, Emperor Wu, China was prospering as it never had before. The Han's focus on agriculture had massively boosted production, which, in turn, had stimulated commerce. Subsequently, commerce encouraged innovation, and Chinese society progressed in astonishing ways. Inventions of this time included paper, the seed drill, the wrought iron manufacturing process, and ocean-going sea vessels (Kerr, 2013).

In the intellectual sphere, there were advances in the fields of astronomy, geology, mathematics, and medicine. Politically, Emperor Wu broke the association of Chinese Emperors with Legalism and enshrined Confucianism as the official court doctrine; inaugurating a position it would hold for more than two millennia. The Confucian classics that had been purged under Qin Shi Huang Di were once again recorded as the Chinese cultural tradition of oral history had saved them for posterity.

Under Emperor Wu, China became strong enough to send punitive military missions out to confront the steppe tribes that continually threatened its borders. The Xiongnu, a major nomad confederacy, were defeated, and China gained control of vast new regions in the northwest. China now directly bordered the cultures of central Asia, and this connection initiated the Silk Road trade route (Cao & Sun, 2011). The years from 202 BCE to 189 CE were considered to be a golden age. So esteemed in fact, that the ethnic Chinese to this day use the name of this dynasty to refer to themselves: the Han.

CHAPTER 3
A UNIFIED CIVILIZATION FRAGMENTS

Visitors to any Chinatown (a common name for neighborhoods with a majority Chinese population) in the world today will no doubt cross paths with a statue of a fearsome warrior. Clad in magnificent robes over metallic armor, he brandishes a fearsome polearm in one hand. Most curiously, his skin is a deep, coppery red, and his eyebrows are large, bushy, and black. His long, black beard flows down across his breast, and he carries an air of authority and regal grandeur.

This hallowed ancestral figure is the image of a man real to history; he is Guan Yu, one of the heroes mythologized in the Chinese classic *Romance of the Three Kingdoms*. The classic

was written in the 14th century, during the Yuan Dynasty, but the events of the book are from an earlier era. Guan Yu was a blood-brother of Liu Bei, and he distinguished himself as a paragon of loyalty and martial virtue during the period's incessant conflict, until his untimely death at the hands of Liu Bei's erstwhile ally, Sun Quan.

The Romance of the Three Kingdoms

The beneficent reign of the first five Emperors of the Han

was not to last. Problems were growing at the bottom, middle, and top of society. The well-being of the peasant farmer, so important to the establishment and prosperity of the Empire, was neglected as taxes rose, causing mass impoverishment. As a consequence, Daoist protest movements, including the *Yellow Turbans* and the *Five Pecks of Rice*, gained popularity amongst the common people. These movements preached that the Emperor had lost the Mandate of Heaven and so rebellion and overthrow of the imperial order were justified (Keay, 2009).

As central control broke down, the fiefdoms grew in power and began to absorb one another. By the year 207 CE, three warlords had established themselves as China's leading military powers and they were on a collision course: Cao Cao, Sun Quan, and Liu Bei. Of the three, Cao Cao was closest to the imperial regime—he was a brilliant statesman who served as Minister of Works under the Emperor. Tasked with quelling revolt and banditry, he used his powers to expand his sphere of influence from within the center of the floundering Han empire. Sun Quan was the son of an official, while Liu Bei was born into poverty. Both had distinguished themselves as supporters of the government, Sun Quan by his military activities against the hill tribes of the south, and Liu Bei by his leading of militias against the Yellow Turbans.

Cao Cao held the upper hand in the conflict, as the court of the Emperor was under his military oversight, and his forces controlled the heartland of China. Victory after victory followed in Cao Cao's campaigns until he was in a position to invade the south of China. A late alliance between Liu Bei and Sun Quan met Cao Cao's superior forces on the banks of the Red Cliffs of the Yangtze. Through brilliant tactics involving fire ships and a surprise marine assault, Liu Bei and Sun Quan were able to defeat Cao Cao's overwhelming army and navy (Zhang, 2015).

Cao Cao retreated to the north, and Sun Quan married his sister Liu Bei to cement their alliance. China had essentially been divided into three. Twelve years after the Battle of the Red Cliffs, Cao Cao's son Cao Pi forced the last of the Han imperial leaders, Emperor Xian, to abdicate, and declared himself the first Emperor of the Wei dynasty. In response, Liu Bei proclaimed himself as Emperor of the Shu dynasty, and Sun Quan named himself the King of Wu (later, he would declare himself Emperor Wu).

These three Empires would remain locked in antagonism until Wei was able to conquer Shu in 263 CE. Before Wei could turn its attention to the state of Wu, however, the dynasty was usurped from within. With echoes of Cao Pi's deposition of the Han Emperor, Sima Yan, head of the powerful Sima clan, forced the abdication of Cao Huan, grandson of Cao Cao, and assumed the title of Emperor of the Jin Dynasty. By 279 CE the Jin Empire had the resources to launch a massive offensive against the state of Wu. Five armies invaded southern China across the Yangtze, in tandem with an armada that swept down the coastline. It was an onslaught that Wu could not withstand and, within months, their Emperor had surrendered (Kerr, 2013). China was unified once more.

The Western Jin

Only thirty years after its founding, Western Jin found itself in a state of crisis. The imperial successor, Emperor Hui, suffered from an inherited disability and, consequently, a power struggle broke out amongst his extended family as they sought for de facto control of the throne. The warring factions of the

Sima family hired mercenaries from the ethnicities that fringed the Chinese world; the Xiongnu, the Jie, the Di, the Qiang, and the Xianbei (Zhang, 2015). Sima Yue emerged victorious from the family struggle, but his victory was won at the cost of a state in crisis.

Fragmentation and Conflict

The peoples who fringed the lands of China, and who populated its highlands and hinterlands, were considered by the ethnic Han to be "barbarians". They were the yardstick by which the ethnic Han measured their own civilizational progress. But in the year 304 CE, the barbarians would achieve their revenge.

Recognizing the weakness of the Jin state, armies led by these tribespeople began to run amok in northern China. In 311 CE, an army led by members of the Xiongnu tribe captured the Jin capital of Luoyang and razed it to the ground, massacring the entire populace and despoiling the graves of the imperial ancestors. Emperor Huai of Jin was killed, but members of his court and family were able to flee, eventually founding a new capital near modern-day Nanjing. This marked the beginning of the Eastern Jin dynasty. Eastern Jin still controlled all of China south of the Yangtze, but to the north and west civilization was in a state of near collapse as the Jie, the Di, the Qiang, and the Xianbei flooded in to join the Xiongnu in declaring their own kingdoms over the ruins of the Jin state (Keay, 2009).

For over one hundred years, wars raged amongst these petty feudal domains of the north, in an era known to posterity as the "Sixteen Kingdoms". The south was not altogether stable too, as the Jin Empire was usurped by the Liu Song Dynasty. Remarkably, this period of chaos did not extinguish the spirit of Chinese culture. The ruling class of the "barbarians" of the north adopted many aspects of Chinese culture, and the mass migration of ethnic-Han into the south led to the region outstripping the north in terms of productivity and technical knowledge for the first time in history (Cao & Sun, 2011). In the north, the new religion of Buddhism, first introduced during the Han dynasty, continued to spread, as did the teachings of Daoism (Kerr, 2013).

Gradually, the north was unified under the Wei dynasty, while the leadership of the south passed from the Liu Song Dynasty to the Southern Qi, then Liang, and finally the Chen. The Wei dynasty fractured into the Northern Qi and Northern Zhou. Just when it seemed that China would be forever divided into two cultural spheres, north and south, a new leader emerged.

The Sui Empire

Yang Jiang was a distinguished official of the Northern Zhou and a member of the extended imperial family. Perhaps tired of the excesses of Emperor Xuan, his son-in-law, and realizing his own superior capabilities, Yang Jiang took advantage of Xuan's early death to seize control of the state, becoming Emperor Wen of Sui.

As Emperor Wen, he immediately exercised his powers to initiate a period of transformation. Legalism was given a place of honor in his court above Confucianism, and his personal religion of Buddhism was heavily patronized. A new system of bureaucracy was instituted, which served as the template of all future Chinese imperial administrations. Wen confiscated large private landholdings and leased them back to the peasantry, collecting taxes on their produce. Alongside this redistribution of land, he initiated the construction of massive granaries to stabilize the price and availability of grain. With the agricultural base of his Empire reestablished, he improved his military in readiness for his ultimate objective: the conquest of the Chen Dynasty of the south.

With the state treasury almost empty, Wen succeeded in wielding a force of overwhelming power against the Chen state. In a strategy reminiscent of the Jin defeat of Wu, more than 500,000 soldiers, supported by thousands of warships, were assembled by the Sui Empire along the northern banks of the Yangtze. Faced with a coordinated assault across such a long front, the Chen Empire soon capitulated, and, for the first time in almost three hundred years, China was reunified (Keay, 2009).

CHAPTER 4
ENTER A GOLDEN AGE

A famous tale from the Tang Dynasty illustrates the unique character of the period:

The Emperor turned to the monk, her face quizzical. "Can you provide an example?" she said.

"Of course," replied Fazang, the monk. He stood plainly before her, his head humbly shaved, his robes pale orange. "I have already prepared a room, please come."

Her curiosity piqued, she stood and followed, dismissing the protests of her courtiers with a wave of her hand.

"See this candle?" Fazang said. "This represents the relationship of the One to the Many."

Walking ahead of her, he placed the candle on a plinth at the center of the darkened room.

Her breath caught in her throat when she realized that the room was full of mirrors, each one reflecting the warm light of the candle.

Smiling, Fazang then placed a polished crystal in front of the candle. It sparkled with a thousand radiant points of light. "And this represents the relationship of the Many to the One."

The above passage shows the female Chinese Emperor questioning a Sogdian monk on the esoteric metaphysics of Indian religion (Talbot, 1991). It is fair to say that such an occurrence was unprecedented in Chinese history.

Founding of the Tang

Emperor Wen of Sui had left the newly reunified Empire in a position of strength, but his son, Emperor Yangdi, was not to reign as wisely. As did his father, Yangdi continued not only to patronize Buddhism and the Arts but also to invest in massive construction projects. The Grand Canal, initiated by his father, was completed, connecting eastern China from Hangzhou in the south to Zhangzhou in the north. To celebrate its completion, Yangdi toured the canal triumphantly at the head of a flotilla of barges tens of miles long.

The Grand Canal had been completed by female forced laborers—the pool of male workers devastated by horrendous casualty rates—and this combination of exploitation of labor and personal extravagance typified his reign. Resentments began to build in the populace, and three massive failed invasions of the state of Goguryeo in what is now Korea led to open rebellion. Yangdi fled to the south of China, where he was assassinated. One of his generals, Li Yuan, took advantage of the power vacuum to declare himself Emperor Gaozu of the Tang dynasty (Wright, 2011).

Early Achievements

Emperor Gaozu busied himself with undoing the harm done to the populace by Emperor Yangdi of Sui. As re-established by Emperor Wen of Sui, the equal fields system of government land distribution was extended across the Empire, ensuring that all available land was cultivated, that the peasantry was financially solvent, and that large private monopolies could not develop. Agricultural innovations including waterwheels and improved plows increased the ease of production, and life for the common people of the Empire became better than ever.

Gaozu's reign lasted for eight years before turbulent events forced his hand. His second son Li Shimin, a man of driving ambition who had helped his father carve out the victory as the Sui dynasty collapsed, had killed two of his brothers and all of their sons. Unable to control his son, and fearful of what he would do next, Gaozu abdicated the throne.

Li Shimin's bloody rise might seem like the prelude to a reign of terror, but as Emperor Taizong of Tang, he proved himself to be an exceptionally capable ruler, perhaps more than any Emperor who had come before him. A student of history, he was driven by a personal mission to build a lasting Empire, unlike that of the Sui that he had helped to overthrow. One of his first acts on ascending the throne was to free 6000 serving girls of the court to allow them to live free lives and marry. He also did away with other costly and frivolous court expenses and spectacles. Taizong continued his father's series of reforms and employed people of merit, regardless of political or ethnic background, to serve as his ministers. In a step that would have had Qin Shi Huang Di, the First Emperor, rolling in his terracotta-lined grave, he allowed his ministers to openly criticize him (Bo, 1991).

It was not only court life that was more open and expressive during Taizong's time, but Chinese society as a whole also became more outward-looking. The Tang Emperors was descended from both "barbarian" nomads and ethnic Han and held both ethnic groups in equal esteem. The capital of the empire, Chang'an, was a metropolis filled with people from all across East Asia and even farther afield. The Japanese and Koreans sent delegations to the Tang capital and were so awed that they took many aspects of Tang society for their own. The southern Korean kingdom of Silla used the Imperial bureaucracy as a template. Kimonos, the tea ceremony, and wood-block printing, so typically Japanese to the modern eye, trace their origin to Tang China. The ancient Japanese capital of Nara was even purpose-built in imitation of Chang'an (Wright, 2011).

Taizong's ambition did not end at improving the lives of the common people, he wanted to put an end to the nomadic depredations that had blighted Chinese history. As a Turkic speaker with Turkic blood, he understood how to defeat the tribes of the steppes. By 630 CE, he had forced the Eastern Turks to acknowledge him as "Heavenly Khan" above their own leadership. He then deployed the Turks along the northern border as a guardian force of the Chinese Empire, using their mobility and aggression to perfect advantage.

Just before Taizong launched his assault on the nomads, one man took advantage of the calm before the storm to journey west. Xuanzang, a monk and brilliant scholar, had become frustrated with the existing translations of Buddhist literature. Xuanzang set off for India, on a horse, and with a drunk guide, on a mission to learn all that he could about the life and teachings of the Buddha. For seventeen years he toured and studied, and, when he finally returned to China, he was one of the most celebrated intellectuals in all of Asia, riding at the head of a baggage train gifted by kings and emperors. His work revolutionized the understanding of Buddhism in East Asia and his life and journey became a celebrated aspect of Chinese culture (Cao & Sun, 2011).

The Reign of Empress Wu

Taizong's son Emperor Gaozung, unlike his father, was not an extroverted leader and fearless warrior; in fact, he was famed for his poor health and timid nature. The person of suitable ambition in the Imperial family at this time was, in fact, his favored consort, Wu. Wu rose steadily, first becoming a full Empress, with her children promoted to be first in line for the throne, then subsequently, making decisions for Emperor Gaozung as his health failed him. When he died, she installed two of her sons in succession as puppet Emperors.

Eventually, her grip on the throne secure, she tired of this charade of regency. In 690 CE, she proclaimed herself Emperor Wu of the Zhou dynasty, becoming China's first, and history's only, female Emperor. Wu continued her forebears' policies of supporting agriculture and silk production and took a hands-on role in the imperial administration, often serving as an examiner herself. In this way, she was able to fill her administration with rising talent drawn from low to middle-status families from across China—people who were more likely to be loyal to her than would the offspring of high-ranking families. China prospered, and the population rose from 3.8 million at the outset of her reign to 6.15 million by its close (Cao & Sun, 2011).

Wu's court was a colorful place, and she took a special interest in the teachings of mystics and sages from many various cultures. The arts were lavishly supported, and Wu herself composed books of poetry. She elevated Daoism's *Dao de Jing* to become the curriculum of the Imperial examinations. She also funded the carving of the Vairocana Buddha at the Longmen Grottoes; an exquisite monument regarded by posterity as the quintessence of Tang-era stonework. Viewing herself as a living savior, Wu's identification with Buddhism was so complete that a famous Buddhist monk called Huaiyi was, rather scandalously, rumored to be her lover (Keay, 2011).

While Emperor Wu was undoubtedly merciless in her subjugation or destruction of all who opposed her, however, we cannot be sure of the truth of her reign, as her histories were written by men, the majority of whom resented her inversion of the Confucian order of things. This is a fact that Wu herself would take in her stride. On hearing the words of the poem, *A Call to Crusade Against Wu Zetian* by Luo Binwang, one of the greatest poets of her day, she smiled, praised the poem's composition, and asked why the court had not hired him (Cao & Sun, 2011).

Late Achievements

The Tang Empire was restored when, aged 81, Emperor Wu's health began to fail her and she was unable to prevent the restoration of the authority of her former puppet ruler son, Emperor Zhongzhong. Her other former puppet ruler son,

Emperor Ruizong, followed in his place, but it was not until Ruizong's son Emperor Xuanzong inherited the throne in 713 CE that the Tang Dynasty would reach its zenith.

The infrastructure projects initiated by the Sui and the following years of good governance of the Tang had led to China becoming the driving force behind Old World trade. Along the Silk Road and through the ports of the south, a variety of goods, people, and ideas flowed into China. In turn, Chinese porcelain and textiles were exported in a circulatory exchange. The Tang Empire was undoubtedly the most advanced and powerful civilization in the world, and its capital Chang'an the largest and most glorious city.

Xuanzong's reign was a celebrated time in Chinese history, however, through poor decision-making towards the end of his

life, he sowed the seeds of the dynasty's eventual demise. He took an interest in one of his son's concubines, Yang Guifei, and gave many special privileges to her and her extended family. When an uprising of Khitan nomads in the northeast threatened the Empire, Xuanzong entrusted too much power to one of Yang Guifei's allies, An Lushan, a general who had excelled in combating the steppe menace (Wright, 2011).

CHAPTER 5

A DYNASTY BESET BY ENEMIES

The 13th century was a time of great change on the steppes, precipitated by the actions of one man:

High on the mountain, he makes his sacrifice; pouring the steaming mare's milk onto the stone like the first rays of the rising sun strike the earth. With his belt and hat drawn humbly round his neck, he offers his total submission, beating his chest and then prostrating himself before the risen sun.

The man's name is Temujin, and on this sacred peak, he has sworn to spend his life embodying the will of Tengri, the Great Sky God.

His destiny is not only to unify the tribes of the Mongols; it is to conquer all under the Sky.

We know such intimate details of Temujin's life because they were recorded in a document known as *The Secret History of the Mongols* (Man, 2014). This warlord would change the destiny not only of the steppe tribes but also that of all Eurasia.

Establishment

A Lushan, Xuanzhong's formerly trusted general, rebelled against the Tang overlordship in the year 755 CE, initiating a period of chaos across China. To combat his rebellion, increased power was devoted to regional military governors, who later were reluctant to relinquish their powers and privileges. In the following century, the inability of the Imperial administration and the corrupt military governors to cope with famine on the Yellow River resulted in a peasant rebellion breaking out under the charismatic leadership of a smuggler named Huang Chao. Huang Chao's bandits plundered their way across China, capturing the southern city of Guangzhou, massacring its foreign merchants. The Tang government was forced to employ steppe nomads to quell Huang Chao's rebellion, and by 907 CE, it had lost all authority. Across China, the governors seized regional power as neighboring tribal unions swept in to contest the spoils. As it had done before in the wake of the collapse of the Western Jin dynasty, China broke apart.

The years 907 CE to 960 CE are known to history as the era of the *Five Dynasties and 10 Kingdoms.* Five states claiming imperial overlordship rose and fell in the north, whereas the south split into dozens of smaller kingdoms. Eventually, this period of incessant conflict was brought to a close when a general from the Zhou Dynasty of the north declared himself Emperor Taizu of the Song. Within nineteen years, Taizu had conquered the kingdoms of the south and China was almost whole again (Keay, 2009).

Hostile Neighbors

The world in which Taizu came to power was not the same world that had been dominated by the Tang. The Khitan, one of the many groups of steppe nomads that fringed the Chinese world, had carved out a state in the northeast, dominating a region that included present-day Beijing, Manchuria, and Mongolia. They declared this state the Liao Empire.

The Liao Empire was not a simple tribal confederacy like its ancient Xiongnu predecessors. Rather, it was a state partly modeled on Chinese culture in control of a largely settled populace, including many ethnic Han. The Liao had nothing to fear from Song China, and in 1004 CE, the Liao Empire launched an invasion.

Emperor Zhenzong, a successor to Emperor Taizong, was able to repel the invasion, but at the cost of a peace treaty that saw Song China paying the Liao Empire 100,000 taels (with one tael equivalent to 50 grams) of silver and 200,000 pieces of silk each year. Shortly after this capitulation, a Tibetan people known as the Tangut seized the area around the northern loop of the Yellow River and declared themselves the Xi Xia Empire.

The former Empire of the Tang was now split between three powerful states. Peace treaties maintained a balance of power, and society in each of the states progressed. Despite the contractual tribute leaving the treasury of Song China each year, the Liao Empire used its wealth to buy products from the Song, stimulating the economies of both Empires. The amount of land under cultivation in the Liao Empire greatly increased, as did its population. The state of Xi Xia expanded irrigation across the desert of the northwest and became a leading center of manufacturing—the technology of its furnaces and the quality of its metalwork were considered without equal. In Song China, the privatization of land enabled a system of land tenancy and contract labor to grow up. With more people than ever free to find employment that suited their particular talents, economic activity boomed across all sectors, and the population peaked at one hundred million (Kerr, 2013).

This era of relative tranquility lasted for a century until events in the steppe tipped the fragile balance.

Northern and Southern Song

The Khitan Liao ruled over many other ethnic groups, including the semi-nomadic Jurchen of what is now known as Manchuria. Resenting the government of their Khitan overlords, the Jurchens rebelled, and by 1120 CE, they had captured the Liao capital and declared their own rulership: the Jin Dynasty.

Sensing the opportunity to land a devastating blow on their Liao rivals, the Song allied themselves with the Jurchen. In a coordinated assault from the north and south, the forces of the Khitan Liao were broken between the hammer of the Jurchen army and the anvil of the Song army. It seemed like a great victory for the Song Empire, but their poor performance during the war—the Khitan Liao had not been broken on the anvil but had instead broken through Song lines and escaped west—had revealed to the Jurchen the weaknesses of the Song administration and its military (Chen, 2018).

In 1125 CE, the Jin Empire swept into Song territory, seized the capital, and captured Qinzong, the Song Emperor. Those members of the Song court who survived the invasion fled south of the Yangtze River, and Zhao Gou, a half-brother to the captured Emperor Qinzong, was installed as Emperor Gaozong. The Southern Song, as they would now be known, were able to hold their territory in the south of China and along the Yangtze River basin against the continued menace of Jin, but the historic heartland of China—the middle and lower Yellow River and the North China Plain—was now lost. For the first time in recorded history, China was ruled over by non-Han ethnic people.

It was perhaps because of this blow that Chinese society in Southern Song times became more insular and introspective. Gone was the love of exotica typified by the Tang, and Chinese society began to reject foreign influences. Buddhism, a foreign religion, lost its place of honor at court, and Confucianism underwent a resurgence. Guided by a series of brilliant thinkers, Neo-Confucianism provided an indigenous Chinese response to the cosmological and metaphysical questions originally posed by Buddhism (Zhang, 2015). Daoism also became more organized, and scripture based as it competed with Buddhist temples for patronage and esteem.

Despite the loss of the north, historically the most advanced and populous area of China, and the ongoing antagonistic relationship with Jin, a society under the Southern Song continued to progress in astonishing ways.

Advances in shipbuilding and navigation meant that ocean-worthy Chinese vessels traded across the South China Sea and the Indian Ocean. Inland waterways were patrolled by boats driven by paddled wheels. To support the volume of long-distance trade, the concept of insurance was invented, as was the act of printing paper currency. Gunpowder had been refined from a curiosity into an effective weapon of war, and the Song army was equipped with fire arrows, fire lances (the progenitor of the handgun), grenades, cannons, and flamethrowers (Kerr, 2013).

New varieties of rice imported from Southeast Asia allowed double or triple harvests, and agricultural output increased to the degree that the market could support millions of people involved in a variety of fields, such as tailors, teachers, craftsmen, physicians, merchants, and entertainers. The average citizen of China was able to enjoy more leisure time, and, perhaps more importantly, had more spending power than ever before; as a consequence, urban life was vibrant, and tea houses, operas, bookshops, markets, and hotels thrived across the land (Cao & Sun, 2011).

At a time when Europe was just emerging from the Early Middle Ages, Southern Song society was undoubtedly the most advanced and prosperous in the world.

The Mongol Terror

The steppes of Eurasia stretch in a band across the Old World, from Manchuria in the east, to Ukraine in the west. Bounded by forests to the north, and deserts and mountain ranges to the south, this area of rolling grassland had for millennia been a highly fluid region where tribes of nomadic horsemen competed for control. The fluidity of these tribal confederacies was a result of the wide-open expanse of the land and the horse lords' nomadic nature. Little did the people of the Southern Song know that, in these northern steppes, a storm was rising. The eye of that storm was a man: born as Temujin yet known to history as Genghis Khan.

At the time of Genghis Khan's birth in 1206 CE, the Mongols were a minor tribe of the far north steppe, under the nominal control of the Jin Dynasty. Temujin, a charismatic leader, and outstanding strategist unified the various tribes of the surrounding steppes and transformed their organization from a collection of tribes into an army united under his command.

It was an army that he immediately put to use, employing its unparalleled maneuverability and potential to wage war across multiple fronts to conduct raids, plundering the vulnerable areas of his more sedentary neighbors. Genghis' warriors would emerge unheralded from the wastelands and deserts, striking a target and then retreating. The Mongol army was entirely mounted, and so it was far too swift to be engaged by any opposition forces that fielded infantry. They were armed with a composite bow that could launch arrows up to 500m, out-ranging, and out-performing Chinese crossbows and fire lances. The Mongols were a superior fighting force, even compared to the elite cavalry of the Xi Xia and Jin (Man, 2014).

Mongol raiders terrorized the Empires of the Tangut and the Jurchen, gaining territory and exacting tribute, but the first nation to fall was Kara Khitai, the Central Asian successor state founded by remnants of the Liao Dynasty. The ruler of Khwarezmia, a powerful Islamic nation on the coast of the

Caspian Sea, then made the mistake of killing a Mongol envoy, and Genghis Khan's attention thus turned westward. So began a fourteen-year military campaign that left the former glory of Khwarezmian civilization in ashes and the Mongols as the uncontested masters of Central Asia.

According to some sources, in 1227 CE, Genghis fell from his horse and succumbed to his injuries (Man, 2014). His death did not mark the end of the Mongol Khanate. Instead, it marked a renewal of the Mongolian will to conquer the world. Ultimately, this desire for conquest and vengeance was carried out by his son and successor, Ogedei.

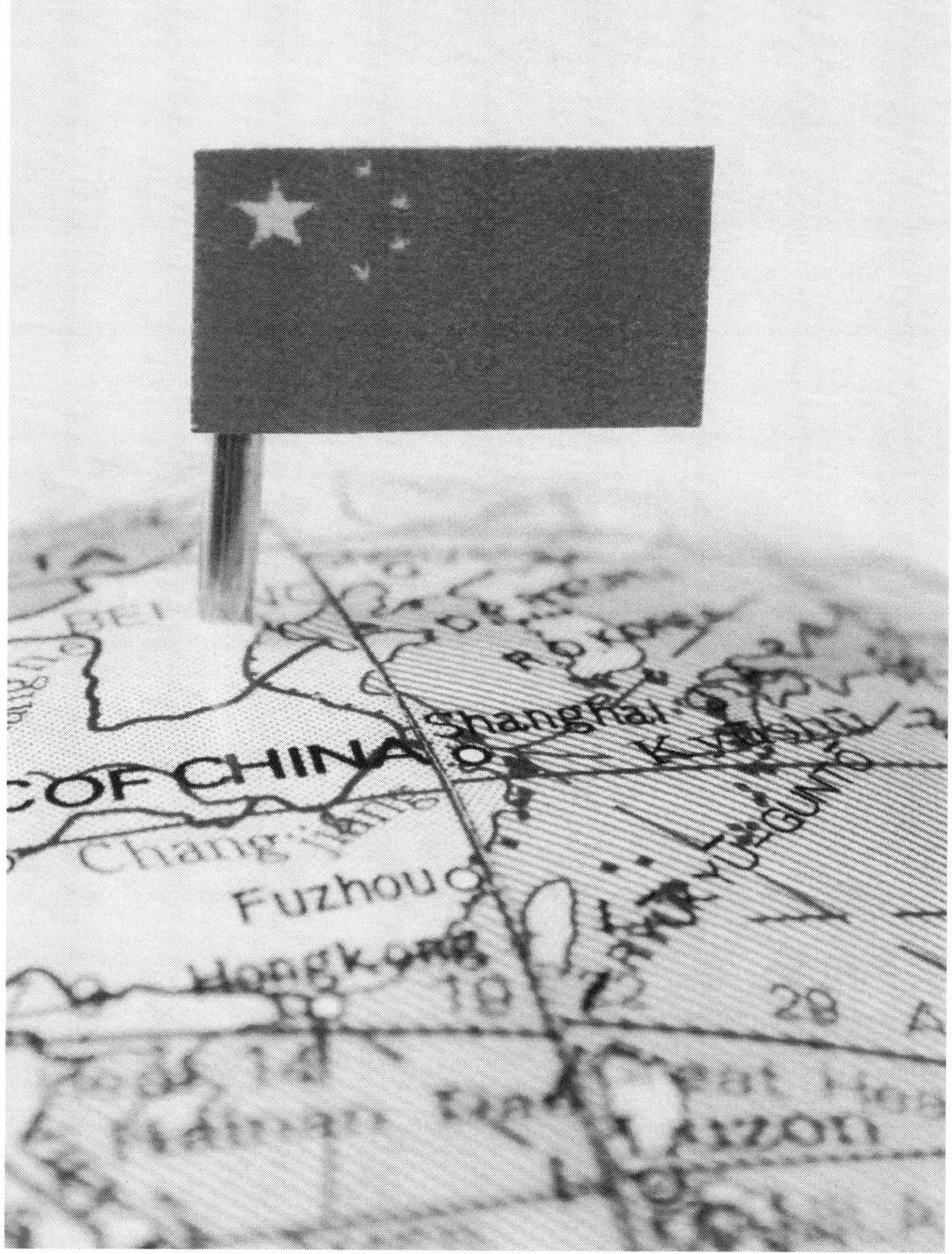
C OF CHINA
Shanghai
Chang
Fuzhou
Hongkong

CHAPTER 6
THE MONGOLS RULE CHINA

n the 13th century, China, or Cathay as it was known to the people of medieval Europe, was a place of utter mystery for Europeans. With direct routes to China blocked either by steppe nomads or the rival civilization of Islam, all Europe knew of China was the exquisite nature of the products that made it along the Silk Road to the markets of Constantinople, Venice, and Rome. Of the realities of life in China itself, they only heard rumors upon rumors. For example, many Europeans erroneously yet legitimately believed that traveling to China would mean crossing a land ruled by people with the heads of dogs (Beazley, 1903).

The veil of mystery separating East from West was torn asunder in a most terrible way, when in 1241 CE, Mongol forces, in the space of only two days, destroyed the armies of both Poland and Hungary. The kingdoms and principalities of Europe were shaken to their core, and the Pope deployed an envoy to meet with the Great Khan, who now ruled an Empire that bordered his own spiritual domain. Giovanni del Carpine, an overweight, middle-aged friar, was given this epic task, and after three months of exhausting travel, he succeeded in reaching the court of the Great Khan at the Karakorum, high on the Mongolian Plateau. Ogodei had died, and del Carpine was able to witness the inauguration of his son, Guyuk, as the new Great Khan. Del Carpine presented Guyuk with a letter from the Pope and extended an invitation to baptize him as a Christian. Guyuk declined, responding that the Pope and all the kings of Europe must come and pay tribute to him, Guyuk, Khan of Khans (Beazley, 1903).

Marco Polo

The Mongol conquest of Asia had created the *Pax Mongolica*; an era of relative peace in the lands ruled by the Great Khan. It was now much simpler for a European to reach the fabled East. One enterprising Venetian family, the Polos, set off in 1271 CE to explore the Silk Road, and, unlike Giovanni del Carpine, reached China proper; after four years of travel, they arrived at Dadu, city of the Great Khan, known in the modern-day as Beijing.

The Polos had not been idle during their long and often interrupted journey across Asia, and by the time they were given an audience with the Great Khan were able to converse with him in Mongolian, his native tongue. This fact, along with young Marco's youth and intelligence, gained the Great Khan's favor, and Marco was employed as an agent and emissary of his government (Bergreen, 2007).

This story may sound like a completely fantastical turn of events—that a lowly merchant from the opposite end of the earth could find a place of high employment under the most powerful ruler in the world—but the policy of the Mongol government was to employ someone ethnically non-Han to oversee the Han. The Mongol population, numbering in the hundreds of thousands, ruled over a Han population numbering in the tens of millions—so, fearing rebellion, they appointed ethnic minorities drawn from across their vast Empire as administrators to aid in their control of the Han majority (Keay, 2009).

Kublai's China

The Great Khan at the time of Marco's arrival in China was Kublai, grandson of Genghis, and the first person of non-Han ethnicity to rule the entirety of China. As Great Khan, Kublai's personal domain stretched from the Pacific Ocean in the east, to Lake Baikal in the north, to Vietnam in the south, to the Pamir mountains in the west. His Khanate was the senior partner in a Mongol confederacy—The Chagatai Khanate, Ilkhanate, and Khanate of the Golden Horde— together made up the largest land Empire in history (Wright, 2011). To an awed young Marco, meeting Kublai was like encountering a living Caesar or Alexander the Great, and this comparison was entirely accurate.

Kublai reigned in splendor from Dadu, his newly constructed capital. It was a city that astonished Marco; a multi-ethnic and multi-religious metropolis filled with the best and brightest from across the huge empire. Unlike European cities of the time, it had not grown up organically—cobbled together in response to the vagaries of war and fortune—nor was it filled with squalor. It had been planned and purpose-built; laid out on a grid with huge, straight, tree-lined avenues. Water flowed systematically through the city's rivers, lakes, and canals, flushing away refuse, cooling the air, and irrigating the land around (Man, 2014).

Within the city were parks filled with rare white animals of all kinds, including stags, squirrels, and ermine. White, symbolizing heaven was the color of Kublai's Yuan Dynasty. Even more spectacular was the palace itself, a fortress within the fortress of a city. Its interior walls were emblazoned with artworks made from silver and gold, and its halls were grand enough to seat thousands of revelers. Even the roofing was spectacular; crystalline tiles shone under the sun, reflecting all the colors of the rainbow.

As an agent of the Great Khan, Marco was able to access this inner world of delights, bearing witness to feasts and festivals on a scale that defied his provincial imagination. Here, Marco engaged in political and theological debates, observed how the country was governed and was left dumbfounded by the sexual stamina of Kublai's attendance to several wives and several *hundred* concubines (Bergreen, 2007).

Marco served under Kublai Khan for 17 years, during which he was sent across China, and to several neighboring countries of Asia, serving as a tax collector and ambassador. On his eventual return to Venice, he dictated the stories of his travels, providing Europe with many details of life in "Cathay". A keen observer, he would provide much information unbelieved by his contemporaries, but corroborated in the light of later knowledge:

"All the people and regions of men who are under his rule gladly take these sheets in payment, because wherever they go they make all their payments with them both for goods and for pearls and for precious stones and for gold and for silver; they can buy everything with them, and they make payment with the sheets of which I have told you."

- Marco Polo (Bergreen, 2007)

For Marco, more impressive than even the extraordinary wealth of the Mongol court was this strange "alchemy" where gold was converted to paper and then back again. It would be another four hundred years before Europe was ready to embrace this particular innovation. Paper currency had been a feature of life in Song dynasty China, but one of Kublai's innovations on ascending the throne was to expand the system throughout his Empire (Man, 2014).

Victory and Consolidation

In 1260 CE, when Kublai became Khan of Khans following a succession conflict with his brother, the Southern Song Dynasty was still intact. Song China, populous, fortified, and possessing a gunpowder-armed army and navy, was a resolute foe. Conquest of the Korean peninsula and the Dali kingdom in what is now the Yunnan province in southwest China enabled Kublai's forces to surround and outflank the Song. After sixteen years of fighting, employing infantry armies composed of Han conscripts, supported by siege engine technology learned from the Ilkhanate's wars in the Middle East, Kublai Khan triumphed.

The Song Dowager Empress surrendered, and Kublai, in a break from Mongol tradition, treated the deposed royal court of the Song well and forbade his armies to massacre the civilians of the Song capital of Lin'an (modern Hangzhou). More intellectually inclined than many of his Mongol contemporaries, and educated from a young age by Chinese luminaries, Kublai saw himself as not only the Khan of Khans but also as the rightful Emperor of China. Taizong, the great Emperor of the Tang, who ruled as both Emperor of the

Chinese and Heavenly Khan of the steppe, was his model for governance, and Kublai set himself the task of building an effective Empire (Bergreen, 2007).

The Mongol postal service—a series of stations served by relay riders—that kept all corners of the great steppe Empire in constant communication with one another was extended across China. Waterways, including the linking of the Grand Canal to Dadu, were improved and extended, as were roads. All currency in circulation was seized and a new Mongol paper currency was issued. In time, three forms of Mongol paper currency were in use in Yuan China, and these currencies were protected against inflation or depreciation by being exchangeable on a 1:1 basis with a set amount of silver or silk. Schools and hospitals were built and a new Imperial Observatory, utilizing the knowledge of the Islamic world, was founded (Man, 2014).

Yuan China was now the driving force and center of a trading network that reached to the ends of Eurasia.

Quest for Expansion

Before becoming Great Khan, Kublai had distinguished

himself as a military strategist during his early years, campaigning against the Southern Song. As Emperor of the Yuan Dynasty, his quest to fulfill his grandfather's vision of Mongol domination of the world did not lessen, and his rule was marked by a series of military campaigns aimed at subjugating all neighboring territories.

Although he was able to comprehensively defeat the Southern Song, the subsequent campaigns launched by Kublai were less successful. Vietnam was invaded three times but managed to repel the Mongols on every occasion. In 1274 CE, an invasion of Japan failed, and in response, Kublai ordered the construction of an even larger invasion force comprising 1,400 boats manned by 140,000 soldiers. In 1281 CE, this fleet attacked the island of Kyushu and the Mongols once again encountered stiff and effective resistance from the Japanese. The two sides were locked in a stalemate when the divine wind or *Kamikaze* arrived—a great typhoon that smashed the Mongol ships to matchwood against the Japanese shore (Bergreen, 2007).

Not only had the Mongol Yuan lost the majority of its naval power, but the aura of Mongol invincibility of the preceding decades had also been shattered. Kublai would only have the will to conduct one more overseas raid; a punitive mission to Java in 1293 CE that also ended in failure.

In 1294 CE, following Kublai's death, the Mongol Yuan became less willing to project their military force. Although diminished, the Khanate was still the world's wealthiest and most powerful civilization. If his successors had taken as much care over internal statecraft as Kublai did, then perhaps the Yuan Dynasty may have endured. As it happened, the Mongol leaders increasingly ruled like parasites on top of a nest; content to live extravagantly on the wealth produced by the Chinese people while becoming less and less invested in the lives and well-being of the regular citizens (Kerr, 2013).

Under the Mongol Yuan, the Han Chinese were essentially second-class citizens. They could not own weapons, and even

access to sharp kitchen implements was limited. The secret police were appointed to every village, watching and listening for signs of revolt, and strict curfews on night-time movements and public gatherings were enforced. Probably most insulting of all for the proud Han people, they were denied access to the machinery of government, as the Mongols preferred to employ non-Han people to administer their Empire whenever possible (Keay, 2009).

Tensions in the populace rose throughout the reign of every subsequent Yuan Emperor, and by 1351 CE, less than a century after Kublai's death, they had reached a breaking point.

CHAPTER 7
THE MIGHTY MING

Aife for the common people during the final years of the Yuan was hard:

Zhu Yuanzhang, aged 16, and his brother buried their father first. They dug the grave themselves, wrapped his emaciated body in white linen, and laid him to rest. Next, they buried their mother, then their younger sister, then their older brother. All laid far below so that the wild dogs would not find them. Each was wrapped in white cloth.

Zhu Yuanzhang and his brother were now alone in the world, but they were not alone—everyone in the valley had spent the winter burying loved ones. Those that could find the strength dug into the cold, hard earth. Some families had gone completely, with no one left to dig the graves.

What now? What to do? Where to go? Perhaps only the Buddha could understand the reason for such suffering.

From the humblest of origins, Zhu Yuanzhang would go on to distinguish himself during this age of great upheaval (Kerr, 2013).

Red Turbans and White Lotus

The early 14th century was a time of crisis in the lands of the Yuan Dynasty. The country was wracked by plague, flood, and famine. One epidemic, lasting from 1331 to 1333 CE, resulted in the deaths of 13 million people. There were further mass outbreaks of disease in the 1340s, 1350s, and 1360s (Sussman, 2011). For the people of the time, it must have seemed like the world was ending, and, as a result, many turned to religion for answers. One sect, the White Lotus, that preached that a Buddhist savior figure was soon to arrive on earth, became especially popular.

In the 1330s, a Buddhist monk and follower of the White Lotus named Peng Yingyu organized an uprising. He was soon caught and executed by the Yuan. Peng Yingyu died, but his adoption of Red Turbans to identify militant members of the sect persisted, and from 1351 CE Red Turban rebellions became common throughout China (Twitchett, 1998).

It was during one such rebellion in 1352 CE that Yuan soldiers burned the monastery of another monk—the now 24-year-old Zhu Yuanzhang. Consequently, he joined the Red Turbans, where his confidence, communication abilities, and intelligence-led to a rapid promotion through the ranks. In 1356 CE, at the head of a peasant army, he captured Nanjing, one of the major cities of southern China.

By 1363 CE, his forces were strong enough to achieve victory in the battle of lake Poyang—perhaps the largest naval battle in recorded history—and his control of the Yangtze River valley was assured. Year by year, Zhu Yuanzhang's forces won victory after victory, extending their territory across China. In 1367 CE, he issued a proclamation stating that the Mongol Yuan had lost the Mandate of Heaven. The statement was a powerful propagandistic victory for Zhu

Yuanzhang and his followers; after all, who could doubt the inauspicious ruination of recent years? Zhu Yuanzhang's epic victories and nascent state-managed on Neo-Confucian principles stood in stark contrast to the weakening, corrupt, and foreign regime of the Mongol Yuan. In 1368 CE, when his armies entered Dadu, they were unopposed, the Yuan court having fled.

Zhu Yuanzhang declared himself Hongwu, Emperor of the Ming (meaning "Bright") Dynasty and set about the task of revitalizing the country. Hongwu understood better than anyone a lot of the peasant class, and he immediately took steps to lessen their burden. The duty of tax collection and law enforcement was assigned to the wealthiest and most senior villagers, lessening corruption. The tax system was overhauled, and tax breaks were given to those who brought uncultivated land into cultivation. Stipulations for a proportion of land to be dedicated to cash crops ensured a supply of materials and finance for the cottage industry. The importance of the Confucian values guiding this reorganization was emphasized, and imperial decrees promoting good and filial conduct were posted in every village and every town across the country.

Confucianism regained its place of dominance at court, and the imperial examination system and method of governance were re-instituted. Wary of the threat of the Yuan court, which still existed in its heartland of Mongolia, Hongwu built a strong military but innovated the process of army selection and assembly so that neither his generals nor their soldiers were stationed together long-term, thus lessening the ability of the generals

to become regional warlords.

Taken solely on the merits of his reign, Hongwu would seem a legendary, almost divine, hero of Chinese culture. But he had a dark side; from the beginning of his rise to power, it became clear that he would kill anyone who opposed him. This fear and paranoia manifested during his reign in the form of much-feared secret police, and a punitive regime with more in common with the excesses of the Legalist first Emperor Qin Shi Huang Di than the Confucian virtues and Buddhist beneficence that Hongwu preached (Kerr, 2013).

China Ascendant

The course of Hongwu's succession did not run smooth, and Hongwu's fourth son seized the throne, becoming Emperor Yongle of the Ming. Like his father before him, Emperor Yongle was a ruthless yet visionary man. He transferred the capital north to Beiping (now known as Beijing), where he began construction of the Forbidden City, a massive imperial palace complex that still stands to this day. The Grand Canal, which had fallen into disrepair in the later years of the Yuan, was renovated, and an extension of the canal was built to supply grain to the capital. With the agricultural base of the country secure, Yongle asserted Ming China's military power, spending many years of his reign at war with Mongol Yuan to the north, and, in a unique period of Chinese dynastic history, projecting the force of China's navy out across the seas (Wright, 2011).

An Age of Exploration

Zheng He was a Muslim man born in Yunnan province, at that time under Mongol Yuan control. During the wars of Ming expansion, he was captured, castrated, and taken to serve by the Ming, being sent to the household of the Prince of Yan. During his time of service, he formed a strong bond with the Prince of Yan, and when the Prince of Yan overthrew his brother and became Yongle Emperor, Zheng He was elevated to the position of Grand Director of the palace.

In 1405 CE, the Emperor commanded that an expedition be set out to explore the western ocean. Zheng He was named Chief Envoy of this maritime mission, commanding 27,000 men and a fleet of 62 treasure ships. On Zheng He's first voyage, he sailed across the Indian Ocean to Sri Lanka and the southern tip of India. Pirate fleets were cleared from the seas, trading posts were established, and an Indian king who had the temerity to resist his diplomacy was captured.

Six such voyages were sponsored by the Yongle Emperor, diplomatically connecting the Ming Dynasty with kingdoms and principalities across Southeast Asia and the Indian Ocean, even as far afield as the eastern coast of Africa. Through these expeditions, Ming military primacy was projected across the known world's oceanic trading networks, extending the Imperial tributary system beyond states immediately neighboring China, and initiating a Ming government-controlled monopoly on international trade was established (Keay, 2009).

Decline Into Crisis

Following the reign of the Yongle Emperor, Chinese civilization took another inward turn. Only one more Treasure Fleet was launched, and thereafter the Ming returned to the non-interventionist foreign policy of their founder, Hongwu. The Mongol Yuan remained a threat, and the Ming increasingly responded with defensive, rather than offensive, strategies—the Great Wall protecting the settled population from the steppe menace took its current form during Ming times (Cao & Sun, 2011).

For over 250 years, the Ming endured, but during that time the achievements of Chinese culture were beginning to be eclipsed by the Europeans as they pursued their Age of Exploration. When one Jesuit missionary at the Imperial court showed the assembly a mechanical clock his Chinese observers were dumbfounded, not realizing that they, the Chinese, had invented the mechanical clock 900 years previously (Kerr, 2013).

Students of China's history will recognize a repeating pattern at the fall of an Imperial dynasty; corrupt officials, an ineffective central government, social catastrophe, and peasant uprisings. All of these factors became apparent in the early 17th century, the final years of Ming reign, perhaps exacerbated by the climate phenomenon known as "The Little Ice Age". During this time, China was subjected to summer droughts, winter freezes, and flooding. Famine broke out, and the Ming government, its treasury empty due to a combination of palace largesse and loss of control of international trade to the European powers, was unable to adequately respond.

In the face of famine, army deserters took to forming large gangs, marauding across the countryside in search of sustenance. The leader of one such group was a peasant named Li Zicheng, who in 1644 CE, marched into Beijing at the head of an army of tens of thousands of disgruntled commoners and ex-militia. Rather than face capture by the rebels, the last Emperor of the Ming Dynasty committed suicide, and Li Zicheng declared himself Emperor of the Shun Dynasty (Cao & Sun, 2011).

It was to be a short reign.

CHAPTER 8

THE MAGNIFICENT QING

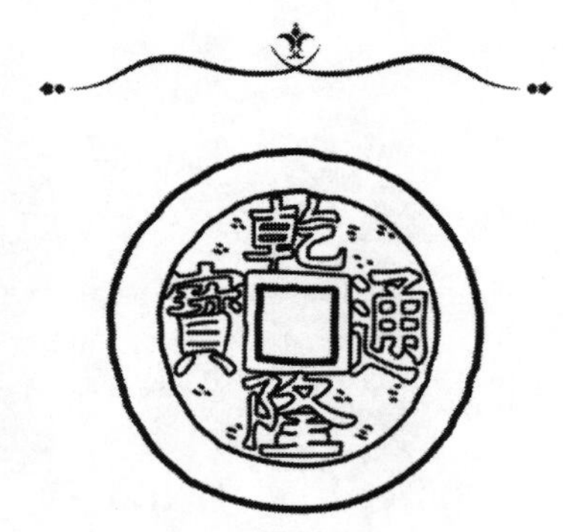

The year 1644 CE saw a Ming general faced with one of the greatest dilemmas in recorded history:

General Wu Sangui stood before the gate. Vast and black it was, spanning the width of the defile between the mountains. From where he stood, it was so large that it blocked out the light of the sun. Wu Sangui perspired. His sworn task was to guard the Ming Empire and its people from the terror that dwelt beyond the gate. The barbarous and merciless enemy on the other side of the Great Wall.

Today, an army stood beyond the gate, just outside. A force of tens of thousands of warriors, flying banners colored yellow, red, white, and blue. General Wu was about to do what he swore he never would. He felt the sweat drip from his chin. With a nod to his men, it was done. They began to turn the winches, and the hinges of the great gate creaked.

A chink of light appeared, widening to a flood.

The gate was open. He had let them through.

Joining the usurping Shun Dynasty or allying with the steppe nomads he was duty-bound to repel, the consequences of General Wu Sangui's choice would echo down through the ages (Kerr, 2013).

The Rise of the Manchus

The freezing cold of the "Little Ice Age" created much hardship for the Jurchen people who lived on the Manchurian plain to the northeast of Ming China. When the Ming state, blind to their suffering, demanded tribute of the usual amount, the Jurchen tribes began to rebel against Ming overlordship. After a period of internecine warfare on the Manchurian plain, one leader had achieved prominence: Nurhaci.

Nurhaci re-organized Jurchen society into four units, each with its own banner and color. These units functioned as both social and military organizations; in an echo of Genghis' exploits, Jurchen society had been fully mobilized for warfare. The Korean Joseon, the Mongols, and the Ming, all felt Nurhaci's wrath and, by 1616 CE, he had carved out a vast amount of territory in the northeast. Nurhaci was now powerful enough to declare himself Khan of the Jin Dynasty (often termed Later Jin to differentiate it from the earlier Jin Dynasty founded by his Jurchen ancestors).

In 1626 CE, Nurhaci died from injuries received in battle with the Ming, but he bequeathed to his sons a strong and well-organized state. His eighth son, Hong Taiji, extended the four banners system into eight, changed the name of the Jin Dynasty to the Qing Dynasty, and renamed the Jurchen people as the Manchu people. When Ming General Wu Sangui opened the gates of the Shanhai pass, Hong Taiji's younger brother, Prince Dorgon, swept through at the head of the most irresistible cavalry force in Asia.

Wu Sangui hoped that he had recruited a powerful ally for the Ming against Li Zicheng's peasant uprising, but the Manchu Qing had other ideas. Hong Taiji's five-year-old ninth son was installed as Shenzhen, first Emperor of the Qing Dynasty, and, reigning as regent, Prince Dorgon oversaw a two-decade-long series of military campaigns that ended in the conquest of the entirety of China (Kerr, 2013).

The Beneficent Reign of Kangxi

Shenzhen's son Kangxi inherited a China restored but not pacified. Many Han Chinese resented the foreign regime of the Qing, and, in 1673 CE, the *Revolt of the Three Feudatories* broke out, led by three Han aristocrats from southern China. Kangxi's forces labored for eight years to crush the rebels, and in the aftermath, he took steps to consolidate Qing control of China and legitimize Qing reign in the eyes of his Han subjects.

By lowering land taxes and prohibiting the practice of land seizure by aristocratic creditors, Kangxi aided the common people. These changes had increased the amount of land under cultivation and stimulated the economy. Indeed, by the late period of his reign, Kangxi was able to free the peasantry completely from land taxation and froze the practice of forced labor.

He promoted, and perhaps more importantly, practiced Confucianism, holding it in a place of esteem at his court. He also commissioned vast works of literature, including a new Chinese dictionary, a grand history of the Ming Dynasty, and the largest book of Chinese poetry ever compiled. As well as patronizing indigenous Chinese culture, Kangxi was open-minded enough to learn from the European diplomats at his court, even becoming the first Chinese Emperor to learn how to play the harpsichord (Kerr, 2013).

This cultural transmission was a two-way street, and details of Chinese civilization learned from returning missionaries and diplomats caused as much of a sensation in Europe as did the brilliant quality of Qing porcelain and textiles. The greatest intellectuals of the European Age of Enlightenment, men such as Voltaire, Hume, and Leibniz, held the philosophies and culture of China in high esteem (Wright, 2011).

Kangxi was a driven man, whose habit of waking early and sleeping late, attending almost constantly to affairs of state, was more similar to that of a 20th century President than that of the pampered autocrats of earlier dynasties. The restored Ming system of imperial administration continued under Kangxi, but he also installed a parallel system whereby regional governors could communicate directly with him; thus, news that would have been filtered out by the imperial administration system under past regimes made its way directly to him, without their knowledge or interference (Spence, 2013).

In addition to being cultured and learned, Kangxi was not afraid to lead; he took personal control of the military campaign against the Dzungars, another group of steppe nomads who had been raiding his northwestern borders and emerged victoriously. During his reign, Taiwan and Mongolia would be incorporated into the Qing Empire, and the growing threat of the Russians, then in the midst of their conquest of Siberia, would be checked by the actions of Qing troops at the Amur River, preventing loss of the Pacific seaboard to the Tsars (Finer, 1999).

When Kangxi died in 1722 CE, Qing China was a huge, populous, multi-ethnic, and rich empire. It was the envy of the European powers whose diplomats flocked to the imperial court—competing for its favor and its trade. It was the envy of the world.

The Glorious Reign of Qianlong

Kangxi's son, Emperor Yongzheng, proved himself as diligent and capable as his father, and his reign was notable for its burgeoning peace and prosperity. His foresight stretched to matters of posterity. When he passed away suddenly in 1735 CE, he had already written the name of his chosen successor within a sealed and locked wooden box. When the box was opened in front of the imperial family, and its contents revealed, rulership was passed to his fourth son, who was enthroned as the Qianlong Emperor.

It soon became apparent that Yongzheng had chosen well, as Qianlong, like his father and grandfather before him, proved a devoted, energetic, and intelligent leader of the vast Empire. He undertook extensive tours of his Empire; on each trip, he was accompanied with beautiful scroll paintings on which he would write notes and poetry. If Europeans had the ideal of the Renaissance man, then Qianlong was the eastern equivalent; beloved by Confucians for his genteel nature and erudition, famed amongst the Manchus for his martial prowess (Kerr, 2013).

Qianlong continued his father and grandfather's campaigns against the Dzungars, eventually extending his domination of the steppe as far as Lake Balkhash in present-day Kazakhstan. Tibet was also incorporated, extending the Empire's domination over more than 4.5 million square miles of territory (Taagepera, 1997). This was more expansive than ever before—and the neighboring states of Nepal, Burma, Siam, Laos, Vietnam, and the Philippines demonstrated their submission by sending yearly tributes to the Qing court.

Qianlong abdicated the throne in order not to reign longer than his beloved grandfather, Kangxi, however, he remained the power behind the throne until his death in 1796 CE. It was during his later years that he would flatly refuse British appeals for a trade deal, and, despite his friendly relationships with western missionaries at court, would remain opposed to Christian expansion within China, as well as being generally suspicious of any outside forces that wished to influence his Empire. Qianlong's attitude to the European trading powers that now encircled his borders would characterize that of his Qing successors (Kerr, 2013).

To the Chinese, the reign of Qianlong was long (the longest, if including his time as retired Emperor) and glorious, but as with all histories, this is the view from a certain perspective. For the Muslim community of China, his reign was noted for lessened opportunities and increased discrimination (Elverskog, 2010), and for the Dzungars, his campaigns were tantamount to genocide (Perdue, 2005).

Encroaching Enemies

General George Macartney, head of the trading mission that was refused by Qianlong, took voluminous notes on life in Qianlong's China, including on the weaknesses of the Qing military as compared to the British. It was knowledge that the

European trading powers, locked in competition for a commercial opportunity, at first did not act upon.

While Qing China was content to sit at the center of a network of foreign tributary states, Europe had been undergoing a transformation from an Age of Discovery to an Age of Empire. The major powers now controlled vast colonial territories and their insatiable industrial economies depended on a constant expansion of colonial extraction. Science and industry had propelled European (and American) military capability beyond the rest of the world, and they were more than willing to use force to solve any disputes that arose in the course of their seemingly never-ending expansion (Cao & Sun, 2011).

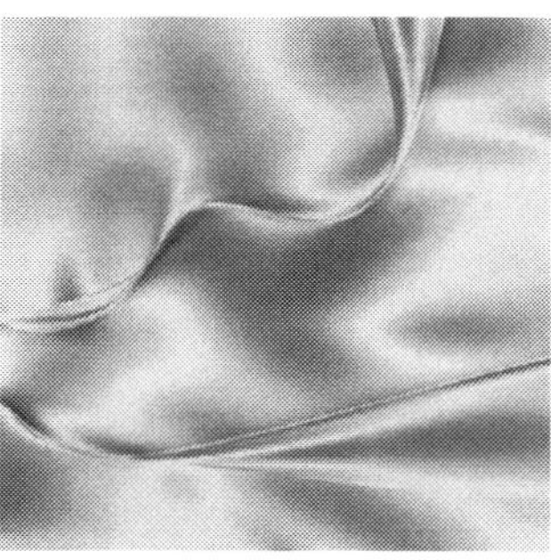

As Europe purchased tea, silk, and porcelain, silver flowed into the Qing Empire's only open port, Canton (now Guangzhou), but the Chinese in turn did not buy any European produce. A trade imbalance grew up, and the British hatched a plan to combat it; they would grow opium in their Indian provinces and turn a blind eye to traders dealing it to China.

The plan worked, and the practice of opium smoking spread throughout the interior of China and across all social classes. Silver, used by the Chinese to purchase opium, began to flow back into British coffers. For those involved in the supply, it was a very profitable enterprise; indeed, when addicted to opium, a life of languor and ruin beckoned. By 1839 CE, the Qing government had seen enough of the detrimental social effects to seize all of the opium found at the port of Guangzhou and throw it into the sea (Cao & Sun, 2011).

In response, the British launched a punitive mission. As George Macartney predicted 40 years prior, the Qing navy proved inadequate against British warships, which now included the ironclad and steam-powered H.M.S. *Nemesis* and the Qing capitulated as Britain seized territory across the south of China. By 1840 CE, Emperor Daoguang was forced to sign the *Treaty of Nanking*, at that point the most humiliating document ever signed by a Chinese Emperor. This document stipulated that a new joint Qing-British tariff system would be introduced and four more ports—Shanghai, Xiamen, Fuzhou, and Ningbo—would be opened to international trade. The island of Hong Kong was leased indefinitely to the British and British subjects in China (and everyone in Hong Kong) could now only be tried for crimes under British law, rather than Chinese law. Britain was also afforded a special status, whereby any future concessions extended to foreign nations would also be extended to Britain. Last but not least, to compensate Britain for the loss of opium in 1839 CE and for the expenses of the war, the Qing government would pay 21 million ounces of silver (Wright, 2011).

As one-sided as it was, the Treaty of Nanking was to be only the first of several declarations signed by the Qing known to the Chinese as the "Unequal Treaties". Opium continued to pour in through the newly opened ports, adding fuel to civil unrest that had been growing since the death of the Qianlong Emperor. In 1851 CE, the instability exploded into a conflict that rapidly spread across China. Hong Xiuquan, a man from the Hakka clan of ethnic Han who lived in southern China, declared himself Heavenly King of the Heavenly Kingdom of Peace. Hong had been influenced by Christian missionaries, and his syncretic vision was of a new China where the evils of Manchu rule and Confucian teachings had been overthrown. With its economy in tatters, its national pride stung by defeat to the British, and the Qing government unable or unwilling to respond to food shortages and the breakdown of law and order, Hong's message found many followers amongst the urban poor (Cao & Sun, 2011).

In one of the lesser-known conflicts of world history, the Qing Empire devolved into a state of civil war. It was an exceedingly bloody war, in which the combatants were equipped with modern weaponry attained through the treaty ports. By 1853 CE, Hong's forces had seized Nanjing and declared it the capital of his new kingdom. Sensing weakness, foreign powers circled like vultures around the ailing Empire. In 1856 CE, the British used a minor incident to incite a full-scale war, beginning the Second Opium War. The Americans and the French joined the British, and by 1860 CE, Beijing had been captured, and the Emperor's Summer Palace burnt to the ground. As with the First Opium War, a defeated China was forced to sign an onerous treaty, ceding yet more of its territory to foreign powers. With this treaty, the British achieved their initial objective of legalizing the opium trade, and at the same time, they legalized the ability of foreign powers to export Chinese citizens as workers—they had managed to turn the people of China into yet another commodity to be exploited, yet more grist for the colonial mill.

The 200-year-old Qing Dynasty was reeling. With the need

for modernization along the lines of the Western powers obvious, ambitious officials and generals who undertook a program of studying and adopting western science, technology, and industry formed the Self-Strengthening Movement. Parallel to this development, a five-year-old Emperor, Emperor Tongzhi, was enthroned and his mother, Empress Dowager Cixi, took hold of the reins of imperial power. In a period known as the Tongzhi restoration, Cixi backed the Self-Strengthening Movement ahead of other court factions, and Qing China began to rebuild. In 1871 CE, the Taiping Rebellion was finally put down, due in part to the modernized military capability of the Self-Strengthened Qing (Keay, 2009).

Unfortunately, Qing China was still suffering. The Taiping Rebellion had devastated the land, and the legalized opium trade now saw society burdened by millions of users and addicts. Meanwhile, tensions were rising in the Korean peninsula, historically a loyal tributary of the Qing. When war broke out with Japan in 1894 CE, the Qing were facing another modernizing Asian state. While the Tongzhi restoration aimed for a modernized military to protect the Empire and its ancient social order, the contemporary Meiji restoration of Japan had seen Japan transform completely in imitation of the European powers, with a constitutional monarchy, education-for-all, and a fully functional industrial base. Partially modern China proved no match for fully modern Japan, and in less than a year the war was over, with Taiwan ceded to the Japanese (Wright, 2011).

Whereas defeat by the British was at least mitigated by their mysterious origins and obviously superior technology, defeat to a member of the East Asian geopolitical order that the Chinese perceived as historically lesser was a devastating blow to the collective Chinese psyche. In response, in 1898 CE, Emperor Guangzhou instituted a series of reforms aimed at modernizing

China as fully as the Meiji restoration had modernized Japan. The reform movement lasted for little more than 103 days before Empress Dowager Cixi backed conservative members of the court and had the Emperor, her nephew, jailed under house arrest (Cao & Sun, 2011).

Amongst the common people, anti-foreign sentiment surged, culminating in the Boxer Rebellion of 1899 CE. The Boxers, named by the Europeans because they practiced martial arts similar to western "boxing", were groups of largely unemployed youth who began to band together to attack what they saw as foreign influences poisoning China; most often Christian missionaries or Chinese converts (Keay, 2009). In 1900 CE, Cixi issued a proclamation in support of the Boxers and their mission to eliminate China of foreign influence, and the movement spread like wildfire. Churches were burned, Christians were massacred, and the diplomatic quarter of Beijing came under siege.

Eventually, a multi-national force was able to liberate the consulates and to occupy the north of China as Cixi and her court, disguised as peasants, fled inland. In the aftermath, the Boxer Protocol was signed in 1901 CE, ceding yet more control of Chinese territory to the assembled interests of Europe, Russia, and Japan, and burdening the Qing treasury with yet more exorbitant war reparations.

A chastened Cixi returned to the capital in 1902 CE, promising social reforms that were never fully realized. She died on November 15, 1908 CE, one day after enthroning her two-year-old grand-nephew as the Xuantong Emperor, and one day after his uncle, the Guangxu Emperor, still under house arrest, had been poisoned to death with arsenic (Kerr, 2013).

U.S.A.
CRAVEN HILL

CHAPTER 9
REVOLUTION AND WORLD WAR

ne of the turning points of 20th-century Chinese history took place in London, England:

Sun Yat-Sen handed the housekeeper his laundry. At least during this captivity, they had allowed him some small courtesies. Given that they had already told him when and how he was going to be killed, it was most probably a pretense at civility—keeping up appearances in front of the non-Chinese staff, people like Mrs. Howe, the housekeeper.

Dr. Sun Yat-Sen was a prisoner inside the Chinese Legation in London, a small diplomatic fragment of the Qing Dynasty within the boundaries of the United Kingdom. The imperial secret service had kidnapped him, bundling him off of the street and into the premises. In a few days' time, he would be secreted onto a ship; returned to China to face show-trial and execution for his revolutionary activities.

His only hope was the note that he had left in his laundry, and his trust in Mrs. Howe's ability to get the message to Sir James Cantlie, his old friend and former medical school professor.

Dr. Sun Yat-Sen, depending on who you asked, was either

China's leading republican intellectual, or a dangerous enemy of the Qing Dynasty (Kerr, 2013).

Sun Yat-Sen and the Revolution

The 19th century was a time of intellectual and political foment in the Western world. Reacting against the exploitation of workers and the domination of hereditary monarchs, nationalist and republican sentiments spread throughout western society. When Marx and Engels published their *Communist Manifesto* in 1858, it gave voice to the yearnings of downtrodden millions. At this time, China was still separated from the west by the barrier of language and culture, and the interior was still largely agrarian rather than industrial. Educated upper-class Chinese, however, and lower to middle-class Chinese involved in trading with foreigners, were able to gain access to the ideas pulsing through Europe, the Americas, and Russia in those times.

One such lower-class Chinese man was Sun Deming, known to history as Sun Yat Sen, an ethnic Han from Guangdong in southern China. Aged 12, he traveled to live in Honolulu, Hawaii, with his elder brother, who paid for his English education. In 1883, Sun returned to China and was further educated in Hong Kong as a western medical doctor. He also was baptized as a Christian at this time and became an active thinker at the head of one of the many republican groups that were growing in response to what they saw as the weakness and backwardness of the Qing Empire.

When China was defeated by Japan in the first Sino-Japanese war, Sun Yat-Sen's mind was made up—an overthrow of the monarchy and founding of a republican government was the only way forward for the nation. He was one of the leaders of a civil uprising in Guangzhou in 1895 that was soon quashed by Qing troops, and he fled into exile overseas (Wright, 2011).

While in exile, Sun continued to develop his thoughts and to correspond with leaders of the republican movement in China. It was during his exile that he was kidnapped by agents of the Qing, and only set free because he had managed to notify Sir James Cantlie of his predicament. Throughout his travels, he continually proselytized for his cause, finding most support from members of the overseas Chinese diaspora, especially those living in Southeast Asia. By 1911, he was the figurehead of a movement that threatened to sweep across China. In October 1911, his supporters initiated the Wuchang Uprising, announcing the new Chinese Republic. The Qing Empire sent General Yuan Shikai, a leader who had rebuilt the Qing army after the humiliation of the Sino-Japanese conflict, to put down the uprising, but instead, the General decided to parlay with its leaders.

When General Yuan returned to Beijing, he had made a deal to replace Sun Yat-Sen as honorary President of the Republic of China. On February 12, 1912, Empress Dowager Longyu had no option but to sign the abdication letter on behalf of the six-year-old Xuantong Emperor. In doing so, two millennia of dynastic Chinese history had ended, and a new Republican era had begun (Cao & Sun, 2011). A democratic national assembly was formed, after which the first election was largely split between a republican faction that supported General Yuan and a coalition of nationalists supporting Sun Yat-Sen who renamed themselves the Kuomintang party (KMT). The Kuomintang, under their parliamentary leader Song Jiaoren, had become the most powerful party under the democratic

arrangement—a state of affairs that the republicans were not willing to tolerate, in March 1913, Song Jiaoren was assassinated, most probably on the orders of Yuan Shikai.

The Kuomintang took up arms but were rapidly defeated by Yuan Shikai's superior forces, and Sun Yat-Sen fled overseas once again. The shining new republic had rapidly devolved into dictatorship. In 1915, when Japan presented its *21 Demands*, an aggressive attempt at subverting China within its sphere of influence, Yuan was able to repulse most of the Japanese ambitions with diplomatic support from the U.S. and Britain. His international standing is now more secure, on December 12, 1915, he declared himself the ruler of a new Empire of China (Kerr, 2013).

Emperor Yuan had badly misread public sentiment, and support for his government immediately began to disintegrate, with even former allies abandoning him. On March 22, 1916, He abdicated his new throne, and, with his health failing, died shortly afterward. China had entered the Warlord Period, as central control completely broke down and regional military governors began to carve up China between themselves (Wright, 2011).

Chang Kai-Shek's China

In the wake of the collapse of Yuan Shikai's regime, the Kuomintang retreated to their heartland in the south. Sun Yat-Sen returned to Guangzhou and, in 1921, set up a military government. Bemoaning the fractured nature of China, Sun Yat-Sen made plans to unify the country by military conquest. His guiding principles of (i) nationalism, (ii) democracy, and (iii) welfare drew broad support from amongst the nationalist groups of China, and he made alliances in order to increase his power base. Most notably, he allied with the newly founded Chinese Communist Party (CCP), enabling him to court alliance with Soviet Russia, then under the control of Vladimir Lenin (Wright, 2011).

One of the men he sent to study with the Russians was his trusted friend Chiang Kai-Shek, a young former soldier who had spent time serving in the Japanese army. Before Sun Yat-Sen could lead his alliance north to recapture the country from the warlords, he died of gallbladder cancer. After a brief power struggle, Chiang Kai-Shek assumed leadership of the KMT and, in 1926, he launched Sun's planned Northern Expedition.

During the expedition, tensions rose between Chiang Kai-Shek's faction and the CCP, and in 1927 he instigated a purge of the Chinese communists, massacring thousands, and instigating the Chinese Civil War. By 1928, the KMT had succeeded in capturing Beijing, and China was once again unified. Chiang Kai-Shek then embarked upon a plan of modernization that was largely a success in the urban and industrial areas of the coastline. In the vast interior, however, rural life was little affected by these changes; with a steadily growing population—that had reached half a billion by 1930—and a static amount of arable land, hardship was, if anything, increasing (Kerr, 2013).

The KMT government lacked control of large areas of this poverty-stricken hinterland, its authority unrecognized either by the warlords, ethnic factions, or CCP guerillas. In September 1931, the weakness of this fragile "Republic of China" was laid bare to the world when the Japanese suddenly launched an invasion and annexation of Manchuria.

Despite this provocation, Chiang Kai-Shek did not risk outright war with Japan and instead focused his attention on defeating the CCP. By 1933, his generals were able to completely surround the Communist-controlled highland area of Jiangxi province, encircling their perimeter with a series of connected fortifications. Calling in air support, Chiang Kai-Shek ordered complete annihilation of the trapped Communists (Wright, 2011).

The Long March of the Communists

On May 4, 1919, a student uprising saw Tiananmen Square filled with protest. Society was changing in the wake of the dismissal of the Emperor, and a China-driven by "science" and governed by "democracy" were the demands of the youth (Cao & Sun, 2011). Only two years previously, a revolution had swept the neighboring state of Russia, promising a world without monarchs and capitalists.

A young man named Mao Zedong was a student in Beijing at this time, and like many of his compatriots, he was searching for answers that would lead to a better China, and a better world. He found these answers in the company of a group of intellectuals who, in July 1921, would find the Chinese Communist Party.

Mao first acted as a secretary for the Party during their time of alliance with the KMT, but this role would rapidly change when the KMT instituted their purges. Mao was appointed Commander-in-Chief of the militant wing of the CCP, the Red Army. After an assault on the city of Changsha failed, Mao and his forces retreated to the mountains of Jiangxi province where they would find their own communist state. Mao oversaw the seizure and redistribution of land from rich landowners and became highly popular with the impoverished peasant class (Wright, 2011).

By 1930, Mao's position was strong enough to attract the leadership of the CCP to join him, who then announced the formation of the "Soviet Republic of China"; an independent communist republic operating within the boundaries of nationalist China. Chiang Kai-Shek responded in 1931 with an encirclement campaign designed to isolate and destroy the communists. Using guerilla tactics, the CCP was at first able to hold off the nationalists, but by 1934, trapped in the center of a fortified ring via the encirclement campaign, the outlook for the "Soviet Republic of China" was bleak.

Spies within the KMT tipped off the CCP leadership that a coordinated land and air campaign was about to begin, and so the Red Army made a desperate attempt to break through the KMT lines. At high cost, 100,000 able-bodied members of the Red Army and CCP were able to escape southwest. Mao's plan was to evade the KMT by traversing the uplands of the interior of China, eventually joining forces with CCP allies in Shaanxi province. From northern China, Mao reasoned, they would be in a better position to liberate Manchuria from the Japanese, and thus, they would win the support of the Chinese public.

So began the Long March, a 370-day journey that took them west across the mountains of southern China, then north along the mountainous edge of the Tibetan plateau, then east across the plains to their destination of Shaanxi, nestled in the loop of the Yellow River. Pursued by KMT forces and their regional allies, exposed to disease and inclement weather, and altogether lacking in food supplies, the march took a devastating toll. Only 10% of those who broke out from the Jiangsu encirclement made it to their final destination, Yan'an (Kerr, 2013).

During the march, Mao's credentials had seen him move from deputy leader to leader of the Communist party with Zhao Enlai and Deng Xiaoping as his deputies. Once in Yan'an, he set about transforming rural society in the same way he had in Jiangxi, and his new power base began to grow (Wright, 2011). Before conflict with the KMT could resume, world events overtook both Mao Zedong and Chiang Kai-Shek.

Japan Invades

Following a minor incident on July 7, 1937, between Chinese nationalist and Japanese soldiers outside of Beijing, the full might of the Japanese war machine was unleashed on China. The Second Sino-Japanese War, and the eastern theater of the Second World War, had begun.

The KMT and CCP signed a truce, theoretically joining forces against the Japanese aggressors. The major cities of Beijing, Shanghai, Nanjing, and, after fierce fighting, Wuhan, rapidly fell to the Japanese and the KMT, like the CCP before them, retreated far inland, moving their government to

Chongqing on the Yangtze River. Red Army counterattacks against the Japanese invasion were highly successful, and their recruitment levels soared (Johnson, 1963). By 1940, hostilities between the KMT had resumed, as the CCP expanded the territory under their control and the KMT fought to contain them. The war against Japan had become a stalemate, but the balance began to tip in China's favor with the entrance of America into the conflict after the 1941 Japanese bombing of Pearl Harbor. Gradually, the Japanese were pushed back, before finally surrendering due to the atomic destruction of Hiroshima and Nagasaki (Wright, 2011).

Civil War Resumes

At the end of World War II, the KMT and CCP were still allies on paper. Further peace talks between the two groups broke down, as the KMT was absolutely opposed to land seizure and redistribution, whereas the communists considered this policy non-negotiable. A 1946 military offensive by the KMT against the CCP was an initial success, but, by 1947, the CCP was able to retake lost ground. China's huge population of rural poor provided an unlimited recruiting pool for the CCP, and the Red Army continued to gain momentum. The Russian Soviet Army, which had occupied Manchuria in the wake of Japan's defeat, ceded it to the CCP, giving them overwhelming control of the north of China, and Mao's troops began to push their way south.

The KMT government was forced to retreat—first to Guangzhou, then Chengdu, until finally, in 1949, Chiang Kai-Shek and his supporters were airlifted to Taiwan. Chiang Kai-Shek's successors in the KMT are, as of 2021, still in control of Taiwan; hence the decades of tension between the CCP controlled mainland and the KMT controlled island.

On October 1, 1949, Mao gave a speech announcing victory in the Civil War from the Tiananmen Gate in Beijing. The People's Republic of China (PRC) was born (Kerr, 2013).

CHAPTER 10

THE PEOPLE'S REPUBLIC OF CHINA

Ahinese civil life would experience unprecedented change under communist rule:

He heard them before he saw them. Their voices raised, their feet frantically pounding the paving stones. Puyi managed to get inside, slam and lock the door behind him. They were coming for him. He climbed the stairs, as fast as his frail, 60-year-old body would allow him, and surveyed the scene from a second-floor window.

There was a group of ten of them or so. Maybe 18 or 19 years old. Just kids. Whether male or female, they were all dressed the same—olive green army fatigues and olive-green caps. Their caps were emblazoned with a bright red star. It wasn't the words they were shouting that pained Puyi's heart, or the fact that they were flinging stones. It was the look on their faces. A fierce scowl that distorted the natural beauty of the young. A look of pure hatred.

Why was this gang of students harassing an elderly, bespectacled librarian? Because of what he stood for. They were Chairman Mao's Red Guards, and he was better known as Xuantong, the Last Emperor of the Qing Dynasty.

As symbolic as it was, this episode was simply one among many—in 1966, all across the country, elders were being harassed and abused by their juniors as China underwent the tumult of Mao's *Cultural Revolution* (Szczepanski, 2019).

Taking The Great Leap Forward

Their control of mainland China assured Mao and the Communist Party began transforming China in their own image. In an echo of the purges that the Communists faced under Chiang Kai-Shek, urban political enemies of the CCP were hunted down, interrogated, and tried. In the countryside, the CCP policy of land seizure and redistribution was extended nationwide. Mao ensured that the peasants themselves, rather than the army, would be involved in delivering the beatings and executions of the landlords; in this way, they became integral actors in the process of the revolution (Kerr, 2013).

Crisis intervened in 1950 when North Korea, then a Soviet Russian protectorate, invaded South Korea, a United Nations protectorate. The United Nations, led by the U.S., staged a counter-invasion that drove the North Korean forces back, mere miles from the border with China. It was at this stage that the Chinese, fearing the arrival of U.S. troops on Chinese soil, intervened, pouring over one million troops into the conflict. The United Nations force was repelled, pushed back to the 38th parallel, the original line of demarcation of the divided country, and an armistice was signed (Wright, 2011).

Bolstered by this surprising success against their natural enemies, imperialist capitalists, the Communist Party was ready to begin its next stage of social transformation. The U.S. and its allies had been angered by the intervention, and a trade embargo confirmed the PRC's status as an international pariah. On the other hand, their relationship with Soviet Russia was stronger than ever, and it was to their Communist brothers that the CCP leadership turned to aid them in the development and execution of their first Five Year Plan. Beginning in 1953, China mass-mobilized its population with the aim of developing a base of heavy industry. In concert with this industrial program, the joining together of farms as collective enterprises was encouraged.

It was a time of great promise for the rural poor, who for the first time in history were given access to free schooling, free healthcare, and even free meals. The demands of collective enterprise also necessitated improved literacy and the development of new skills. This period of the 1950s could be called "Mao's Golden Age"—it even included a brief period of political openness in 1956 called "The Hundred Flowers Campaign" where people were mandated to criticize mistakes made by the Communist Government in writing (Keay, 2009).

By 1957, the perhaps too-criticized Mao had reneged on the spirit of openness; using the evidence provided by the recorded criticisms, he mercilessly purged opponents of the CCP from society. Maoism had taken a greater grip on life in China, and he now forged ahead with his Second Five Year Plan. This was not to be a plan on the Russian model, this was to be an indigenously developed plan to make use of China's greatest resource: its prodigious supply of rural labor.

The farming collectives across China were merged into even larger units known as communes. These communes were both agricultural and industrial. Every commune built at least one kiln in which to process metals. With hundreds of thousands of kilns in place throughout the vast country, surely it would be a simple task to achieve Mao's goal of equaling Britain's steel output (Wright, 2011). As it happened, the primitive kilns with their inadequate material inputs could not even produce steel, let alone match the output of any major industrial nation. As disappointing as this must have been for the CCP leadership, of far more concern was the effect the policies were having on agricultural production. In the fervor to achieve the stated objectives of the Second Five Year Plan, records were being falsified and yields were being over-reported at all levels; from the farm laborer to the high administrators. The grain that did actually enter the communal granaries was then prioritized in its distribution to the cities, rather than to the villagers who had grown it, with some even being sent overseas to pay off debts (Keay, 2009).

The upper leadership of the CCP was either not willing or not able to believe the catastrophe unfolding on their doorstep, and late 1950s and early 1960's China—with food restrictions exacerbated by a flooding Yellow River and countrywide pest outbreaks—was a time of massive famine. One Communist Party member dispatched to the provinces described dead bodies piled up in every village he visited. These bodies were half-eaten. When he questioned the villagers on what had happened to the dead, they answered that the dogs had been eating them. He knew this to be a lie because the dogs themselves had all been eaten many months before (Jisheng, 2012).

It was a tragedy that took the lives of untold tens of millions, most likely the worst famine in human history, and altogether the setback was one that not even a near-deified leader like Mao could ride out. Tensions with Soviet Russia had also risen, with the Chinese disappointed by what they saw as a movement away from Marxism in the wake of Stalin's death, while the Russians for their part were aghast at Mao's cavalier attitude to the dangers of nuclear conflict:

"China has many people. They cannot be bombed out of existence ...

The deaths of 10 or 20 million people are nothing to be afraid of."

- Mao Zedong (quoted in Li, 1994)

Mao resigned as Chairman of the People's Republic of China and retreated from frontline politics, while still remaining the paramount leader of the country as head of the military and Chairman of the Communist Party (Keay, 2009).

The Cultural Revolution

Now adrift in the international wilderness, China took a more pragmatic turn as two other veterans of the Long March assumed frontline leadership: Zhou Enlai and Deng Xiaoping. Zhou was a longtime supporter of Mao, but a moderating influence both on Mao and other members of the party, while Deng was a realist, who valued results on the ground over political theorizing. Deng's philosophy could be summarized by an old Chinese parable that he was fond of quoting: "it doesn't matter if the cat is black or white, if it catches mice, it is a good cat" (MacFarquhar & Schoenhals, 2008). Grain was imported to help ease the famine, the collectives were disbanded, and small-scale market activity was allowed to resume. Slowly, China began to recover (Wright, 2011).

This liberalizing influence, however, was not going to last. In 1966, Mao returned from his period of introspection, determined to re-stamp his authority on the party and on China. To Mao, those who had appropriated leadership of the Communist Party from him were nothing less than a new bourgeoisie rising up to dominate the proletariat; "capitalist roaders," putting China on course to follow what he saw as Russian Soviet capitulation to the West. According to Mao, what was needed was for the younger generations to experience a return to the origins of the revolutionary struggle (Keay, 2009).

To this end, he called for "The Great Proletarian Cultural Revolution". A working committee composed of his most dedicated followers was set up to guide the movement, and a sycophantic general, Lin Biao, was promoted to the twin positions of Vice Chairman of the Communist Party of China and Vice President of the People's Republic of China. It was Lin Biao who had compiled and published the famed *Little*

Red Book of Mao's sayings that would go on to play such a central role in the upcoming upheaval (Wright, 2011).

Mao began to publicly censure his opponents in the Communist Party as his supporters became active amongst student groups across China. Mao lauded these student groups, proclaiming them his "Red Guards" and a tinderbox was lit across China. By August 1966, mass rallies were being held in Beijing, where Mao appeared in front of millions of red-clad students who brandished his *Little Red Book* aloft while fervently chanting revolutionary slogans. Mao told them that proletarian authority in China was being usurped by "intellectuals and counter-revolutionaries," in schools, universities, and even the Communist Party itself. Rebellion against these forces was therefore justified under Mao's rhetoric.

The mass hysteria grew, and gangs of Red Guards spontaneously sprang up across the whole country, attacking everything that spoke to them of China's history, bourgeois rule, or counter-revolution. Ancient temples were vandalized, priceless heirlooms smashed, and precious artwork destroyed. Far more distressing, lives were also destroyed—across China, teachers were pulled from their classrooms, doctors from their surgeries, officials from their posts. The fanatical Red Guards then proceeded to "re-educate" their victims; criticizing them, spitting on them, beating them, forcing them to admit to political thought crimes. The lucky were sent to labor in the fields with the peasants, the unlucky to the grave (Wright, 2011).

To foreign observers, it was an outbreak of collective madness. Realizing that he was losing control of the movement, Mao ordered the army to act. The Red Guards were rounded up and, in a bizarre twist of fate, sent to the countryside to join the people they had recently denounced in forced rural manual labor.

It was not until Mao's health began to fail in the mid-1970s that a thaw in the culture of mutual suspicion and paranoia appeared. By that time, Mao's former anointed successor, Lin Biao, had mysteriously died in a plane crash while attempting to flee China. Political power was now concentrated in the hands of Mao loyalists known as the "Gang of Four"—Mao's fourth wife, Jiang Qing, and her associates Zhang Chunqiao, Yao Wenyuan, and Wang Hongwen. The moderating influence of Zhou Enlai ended with his death in January 1976, and Mao followed soon after in September of that year.

Before he passed, Mao was able to install the next paramount leader of China: a hardline Maoist known as Hua Guofeng (Keay, 2009). The "Gang of Four" meanwhile, began a purge of moderates, including that most progressive member of the party: Deng Xiaoping.

An Era of Modernization

While Hua Guofeng was a Maoist, he was also a pragmatist; he saw the Gang of Four as dangerous radicals who were likely to challenge his leadership. Having gained the trust of the military in the weeks following Mao's death, he quickly made his move. On October 6, 1976, the Gang of Four were summoned to an emergency meeting where, much to their surprise, they were promptly arrested. In later televised show trials, the four were found guilty of instigating the Cultural Revolution and jailed for life (Wright, 2011).

Hua Guofeng then acted to rehabilitate Deng Xiaoping and other moderates and modernizers within the party, and

Chinese society exhaled a collective breath of relief. The chaos of the Cultural Revolution was assigned to the past, the blame pinned squarely on Lin Biao and the Gang of Four, and once again China began to rebuild. Deng Xiaoping counseled a return to the policies that had served him and his late ally Zhou Enlai so well pre-Cultural Revolution: the "Four Modernizations." That is, the modernization of agriculture, industry, defense, and technology (Keay, 2009).

The communes were dismantled, and in the countryside, small-scale markets were allowed to resume. Infrastructure was improved, and credit and energy supplies became more readily available. Steps were also made to combat ongoing exponential population growth—by 1976 CE, China had reached a population of 930 million—with an official (but in practice often unenforceable) one-child policy. Deng Xiaoping, the canny political veteran, was the driving force behind these changes, and by 1980, he had replaced Hua Guofeng as the paramount leader of China (Wright, 2011).

Under Deng's leadership, Communist China embarked upon an unprecedented experiment with capitalism. Special Economic Zones (SEZs) were opened up along the coast, where local authorities were free to adjust laws and taxation to attract foreign investment and were encouraged to enter into partnerships with foreign enterprises. In 1984 CE, these four zones were followed by fourteen more, and soon after the majority of the eastern seaboard was open for business. To lessen the burden of numbers on the state and on the ecology of China, the one-child policy was tightened (Wright, 2011). In tandem with these changes, steps were made to rehabilitate China's international reputation.

The alliance with capitalism and a new level of international openness, however, did not extend to the practice of democracy. Even as it appeared to modernize in the eyes of the world, the Communist Party continued to increase its level of control of the population. When frustrated student protests broke out in 1989, chanting the same slogans of the days of Mao's 1919 youth, "science and democracy!" martial law was declared and the spirit and bodies of youths crushed under the wheels of tanks (Wright, 2011).

China Transforms

The Tiananmen Square massacre shocked the world, and China almost found itself in the international wilderness once again. While the nations of the West protested, they did not fully cut ties with China. The tendrils of capitalism were now too deeply rooted; China and the west found themselves linked in an economic system of mutual dependence. It was now "the workshop of the world," and the international market was desperate for the products of that workshop (Kerr, 2013). The West may have placed an arms embargo on China, but they did not go so far as to liquidize their significant investments.

In the wake of the crackdown on democracy, the

movement towards a more modern country stalled until 1992, when then retired Deng Xiaoping made a tour of southern China. On this tour of the SEZs, he publicly reiterated the importance of the economic reforms that he had begun in the late 1970s. Jiang Zemin, his successor at the head of the party, took heed of the elder statesman's counsel, and so began the next stage of the modernization of the Chinese economy (Zhao, 1993).

After 1992, the pace of economic liberalization accelerated; state industries were privatized, tariffs and other barriers to international trade were reduced, and China became a member of the World Trade Organization. The SEZs were extended to the inland capitals of the major provinces, and to paraphrase Deng, getting rich was now considered to be glorious (Whiteley, 2007).

This hybrid socialist-capitalist system, or "Socialism with Chinese characteristics," pioneered by Deng Xiaoping, and continued by his successors, has transformed China in remarkable ways (Wright, 2011). In 1981, according to the World Bank, 90% of the population of China lived in absolute poverty, but by 2013, this figure was down to only 2%. The average citizen did not only move out of poverty during this time, they moved into prosperity, with per capita GDP growing by over 23 times in the period from 1978 to 2017 (qz.com).

From lacking basic infrastructure in 1978, China now leads the world in the construction of steel, ships, concrete, and textiles (Rawski, 2008). Even as the economy shifted away from agriculture, farmers still benefited from government support, with farming incredibly becoming exempt from taxation in 2005. Literacy now exceeds 97% of the population, and life expectancy has risen from only 40 years in 1940 to 76 years in 2019 (Kerr, 2013).

In 1997, Hong Kong was returned to China along with Macau in 1999 as China's international status burgeoned. Jiang Zemin's successor, Hu Jintao, adopted the "soft power" approach to international affairs, favoring openness, alliances, and investment over military coercion and economic threats. Hu Jintao's successor, Xi Jinping, built on the foundations of Hu Jintao's soft power era by beginning the construction of "Belt and Road Initiative", a series of foreign development partnerships that are building a 21st century equivalent of the ancient land and sea Silk Roads; connecting the markets and materials of both Eurasia and Africa together, with China as the lynchpin in the network (Morrison, 2019).

As of 2021, China is the world's second-biggest economy and is on course to overtake America in the next decade. It has the world's most valuable internet, mobile phone, and automobile markets and the world's largest holdings of foreign exchange reserves. In terms of manpower, its military is first in the world, only lagging behind the U.S. and Russia when the technological capability is accounted for. That technological gap is narrowing China is currently forging ahead with an ambitious manned space program, and has already sent unmanned vehicles to the Moon and Mars (nytimes.com).

Sitting at the center of the "Belt and Road", China is once more the Middle Kingdom; the crossroads and driving force of world trade and industry. Conditions are already in place to ensure that the 21st century will be China's century, but it remains to be seen what path the Chinese will take. As past imperial history has shown, negotiating the future is a delicate balancing act.

While progress has been made in health, wealth, and education, and the population stabilized, the unforeseen complication of a narrowing demographic pyramid has shrunk its labor pool, tax base, and disrupted its ratio of males to females. Thanks to the consequences of technology and heavy industry, the Chinese environment now suffers under a heavier burden than ever before (Kerr, 2013). While China has become a technological, industrial, and military leader, its political system remains resolutely undemocratic, with restrictions on information technology, the media, and free speech, under the auspices of a steadily developing surveillance state. Indeed, international concerns have been raised over the "vocational education and training centers" employed to contain and control ethnic Uyghurs in Xinjiang province (Canadian House of Commons, 2020).

China's rise to international pre-eminence was developed largely through "soft power", but under Xi Jinping, China has been more willing to use old-fashioned "hard power", as seen by its building of military bases in the South China Sea and its increased willingness to engage in border skirmishes. The future is not certain. In the globalized world of today, China's coming rise or fall will not just affect the Han people; it will affect us all.

CONCLUSION

China's history is an incredible tale of inspiration, fortitude, ambition, chaos, and courage. Beginning from an era of myth and legend, archeological evidence reveals to us that it was one of the cradles of human civilization, developing independently from other comparable early civilizations such as the fertile crescent of the Middle East, the Indus Valley, or the western seaboard of Peru. Unlike these other civilizations of antiquity, Chinese culture—although undergoing cycles of rising, equilibrium, and collapse—continues to develop in response to internal and external pressures.

Our journey proceeded in five broad steps: reviewing the events, key personalities, and achievements of the five major eras of Chinese history:

Ancient China (pre-221 BCE)

From the mists of time emerges the Shang writing system: the direct antecedent of the modern Chinese script and language. The Shang dynasty is where archeology draws the boundary of the recorded history of China, and Shang society is revealed to possess many of the core cultural qualities that we recognize today as "Chinese", such as pictographic writing, the manufacture of silk, the working of jade, and the religious veneration of ancestors (Keay, 2009).

Shang society progressed to Zhou society, and in this feudal era, we saw the emergence of the classic philosophies of China, including Daoism and Confucianism. Civil and cultural life blossomed, but the authority of Zhou kingship was usurped as regional rulers began to war against one another.

The First Imperial Age (221 BCE to 580 CE)

The first imperial age stretches from the unification of the warring states under the rulership of the Qin, through China's first "golden age" under the Han, to a long period of collapse and fragmentation that threatened to put an end to Chinese unity. This era saw the initial stages of what was to become The Great Wall, as well as the beginnings of the overland and maritime "Silk Roads" that would connect the economies of Europe and China, with some periods of interruption, to the present day.

The Second Imperial Age (581 CE to 1270 CE)

The Second Imperial Age begins from the reunification of China under the Sui Dynasty, followed soon after by the establishment of the Tang Dynasty—China's second golden age; a time when the nation greatly expanded its borders and became enraptured of foreign influences, including the Indian religion of Buddhism, and the fruits of the trade from the Silk Road. China also exported its own high culture to Japan, Korea, and Vietnam during this era. After another period of near-collapse, China under the Song Dynasty prospered until enemies from the steppes took control.

The Third Imperial Age (1271 CE to 1911 CE)

The rule of the Mongol Yuan marks the beginning of the

third age of imperial history. As the Mongols were foreigners, their dynasty proved unpopular and was eventually overthrown by the native Han-led Ming. Under the Ming Dynasty, China demonstrated a seagoing potential capable of outstripping the burgeoning European Age of Discovery, but instead, the Chinese took an insular turn, halting their voyages of exploration. After a period of misgovernance and natural disaster, another tribe of foreigners seized the Empire—this was the Manchu-led Qing Dynasty, during which China once more experienced a period of great achievement and prosperity.

The Modern Age (1912 CE to present)

The "Unequal Treaties" forced on the declining Qing Dynasty by Europe, the U.S., and Japan precipitated a crisis in the national consciousness of China, leading to the overthrow of the Empire and the establishment of a republic. This road to revolution was rocky and perilous, and fierce conflict between nationalists and communists was interrupted only by the Japanese invasion; an invasion that marked the onset of the eastern theater of World War II. After the war, and a final, bloody, struggle, the communists emerged victoriously. Their reign was to witness extreme crises, in the form of the *Great Chinese Famine* and the *Cultural Revolution*, before the nation rallied—undergoing a period of modernization and a resultant spectacular social, economic, and political rise.

Now that you have completed this journey, you have been informed of the mythology, the culture, the philosophy, the science, and the achievements of Chinese history. You are aware of great personages like Emperor Wu,

Mao Zedong, Qin Shi Huangdi, and Confucius. You have witnessed how these and other luminaries, survived, failed, or prospered amid a variety of "interesting times". You have learned about the taming of mighty rivers and the digging of country-spanning canals, the development of extraordinarily productive agriculture, and treasure-bearing journeys across the oceans. You have been enlightened of thrilling court intrigues, secret societies preaching rebellion, and the depredations of the menacing tribes of the hinterlands and steppes.

You are now better equipped to understand the geography of China, the culture of the ethnic Han and the other ethnic groups that make up its population, China's recent history of intense civil conflict, and its recent emergence as a modern world superpower.

All of this is important because China's history is part of world history. Once upon a time, the course of the successive rise and fall of Chinese dynasties was remote and inaccessible to people in the western hemisphere. Now, Western economic destiny is interwoven with that of China—we buy clothes made in China, use electronics made in China, and travel in machines made in China. In turn, we sell the fruits of our own commerce, culture, and industry to China. The People's Republic of China is currently the majority holder of U.S. treasury bonds, and it has the largest military in the world. Its huge demand for energy and materials is bringing it into increasing conflict with other nations, with flashpoints in the South China Sea and the outer archipelagos of Japan, even as its leadership endeavors to negotiate peaceful international outcomes.

Are we witnessing the beginning of a new golden age for the Chinese, like that of the mighty Han or magnificent Tang?

Or are we seeing signs of the beginning of an end—those times when the social fabric begins to fray as economic and ecological disasters overtake central control? China's future stability and prosperity will enable the future stability and prosperity of the entire world. China's collapse, on the other hand, would spell disaster for us all.

This was the history of China. This is **History Brought Alive**.

PRONUNCIATION GUIDE

Chinese symbols representing whole words are commonly translated into a series of Roman characters according to a special pronunciation system. This pronunciation system is different from that used by an English speaker to read Roman characters.

Here are the major differences between English and Romanized Chinese (Pinyin):

Pinyin	Pronunciation Rule
z	pronounced "dz"
Zh	pronounced "j"
Q	similar to "ch", but curling the tongue
X	similar to "sh", but curling the tongue
C	pronounced "ts"
Chi	the ending "i" is pronounced "err"
Shi	the ending "i" is pronounced "err"
Zhi	the ending "i" is pronounced "err"

(Source: Upton-McLaughlin, 2013)

TIMELINE

Xia Dynasty	2070–1600 BCE (unverified)
Shang Dynasty	1600–1046 BCE
Western Zhou Dynasty	1046–771 BCE
Spring and Autumn Period	770–476 BCE
Warring States Period	475–221 BCE
Qin Dynasty	221–206 BCE
Western Han Dynasty	206 BCE–8 CE
Eastern Han Dynasty	25–220 CE
Three Kingdoms	220–280 CE
Western Jin Dynasty	226–316 CE
Eastern Jin Dynasty	317–420 CE
Northern and Southern Dynasties	420–589 CE
Sui Dynasty	581–618 CE
Tang Dynasty	618–907 CE
Five Dynasties and Ten Kingdoms	907–960 CE

Northern Song Dynasty	960–1127 CE
Southern Song Dynasty	1127–1276 CE
Yuan Dynasty	1271–1368 CE
Ming Dynasty	1368–1644 CE
Qing Dynasty	1636–1911 CE
Republic of China	1912–1949 CE *continues in Taiwan
People's Republic of China	1949–present

(Source: Cao & Sun, 2011)

END NOTE

If you have benefited from or enjoyed reading this concise and comprehensive journey through five millennia of China's history, please pass on those benefits and that enjoyment to others by leaving a review.

Thank you for your purchase. Don't forget to check out the rest of the cornucopia of myths, legends, and histories from around the world in the **History Brought Alive** series.

JAPANESE HISTORY

INTRODUCTION

Japan is a fascinating country with a long and storied history. While there are many books that explore Japan's unique history, few offer a complete and thorough explanation of this nation's history that is still readable and enjoyable. Many books try to do too much with too few pages. Oftentimes, important periods seem rushed or lack clarity. This unfortunately leaves the reader with a feeling of incompleteness. These books can also be hopelessly dry, overly academic, and just downright difficult to follow. Some authors even pad their books with unnecessary fluff and filler that serves only to distract from the juiciest details.

Fortunately, this isn't one of those books. This is History Brought Alive! In the pages that follow, you'll find tightly written and poignant information presented without bias. We strive to offer you a refreshing read with reliable, well-referenced information. This concise history will respect your time by getting right to the point and giving you the information, you came to learn.

We'll cover the most important parts of Japanese history, making this a must-have in your library. This book will serve as a reference guide for both scholars and history enthusiasts alike. We'll boil tens of thousands of years down to the essentials you need to know. After all, learning Japanese history ought to be enjoyable.

Why waste time with inferior books that will only confuse you and leave you with more questions than answers. Discover history the way it should be told, with History Brought Alive!

CHAPTER 1
EARLY JAPAN

Japan's storied history stretches back far before recorded history. The islands were a prime spot for early humans to find all manner of food and resources. There are some unique features that made this location ideal for early settlers.

Firstly, there are over 100 active volcanoes across Japan. This is about 10% of all the active volcanoes on the planet. This is due to the fact that Japan is situated upon the meeting point of two massive tectonic plates that form a horseshoe shape. This area is referred to as the Pacific Ring of Fire. It is known for earthquakes and volcanic activity which may sound like it would dissuade humans from visiting, much less settling there. However, there is a major benefit to living in a location like this. As we see in other volcanically formed archipelagos like Hawaii, the ash distributed by eruptions improved the fertility of the soil. Ash contains minerals that weather into the soil and nourish plants. Subsequently, a variety of edible plants for humans and animals alike flourished. The forests that grew here also provided a habitat for a variety of wild game which humans could hunt for food, hides, and other useful resources.

Secondly, Japan is an island chain. This provided natural protection from invasion as well as access to fishing in the bountiful seas surrounding the islands. Fish would become an important staple for Japan's earliest humans.

The First People

Paleolithic People

Some archeologists believe the history of human habitation of the Japanese archipelago could date back as far as 100,000 years. However, as with most of human history from long ago, there's not much in the way of tangible evidence. As we mentioned above, The Japanese archipelago would have made an attractive spot to early humans living on nearby islands or the mainland of Southeast Asia. So, it makes sense to assume human habitation of Japan goes back a long, long time.

The study of Paleolithic Japan relies heavily on stratigraphy or the study of soil layers. The volcanoes of Japan are quite helpful to archeologists since eruptions would cover the soil of the island with levels of volcanic ash which are easy to detect and useful as a reference for establishing dates.

The earliest human remains discovered in Japan were found in the Yamashita Caves in modern-day Okinawa. Archeologists found tools made of deer horns and bones along with the remains of a 7-year-old girl. Carbon dating revealed these to be around 32,000 years old, making them the first physical evidence we have of human habitation in the archipelago.

Around that time, there was an ice age which created lower sea levels. This in turn created land bridges that early settlers were able to walk across. One land bridge to the north connected the island of Sakhalin to Hokkaido. Another connected the Ryukyu Islands with Taiwan to the south. The lower sea levels also mean the Korea Strait was significantly narrower than it is today, making it another route ancient peoples may have used to reach Japan.

It is unclear whether or not the peoples who settled in Japan at this time are the ancestors of modern Japanese people. It is possible that they are, having assimilated with later groups that migrated here. It is equally likely that they died off and are not the ancestors of the modern Japanese.

Whether they are a part of the lineage of the modern-day Japanese or not, it is worth noting they were responsible for the creation of some of the first ground and polished stone tools in the world, dating back to around 30,000 BCE. In most of the rest of the world, comparable tools would not be seen until around 10,000 BCE.

The most prevalent theory is that the earliest ancestors of modern Japanese people arrived in two waves of migration. The first migration is a group of people called the Jomon. The second group of people is known as the Yayoi. Let's take a look at them now.

The Jomon

The Jomon Period spans from around 14,500 BCE to around 300 BCE. In the early Jomon Period, there are estimated to have been roughly 20,000 people living in the Japanese archipelago. They subsisted largely through hunting and gathering.

By the middle Jomon Periods, the population exploded to around 260,000 people. At this point, they had reached a high level of cultural complexity as evidenced by their elaborate tool making and jewelry made of stone, bone, and shells. They carved boats from tree trunks and used them for fishing and traveling, though it is unclear if they used sails or paddles.

Two of the biggest technological advances created by the Jomon People were the bow and arrow and pottery. These appear to have been invented independently by the Jomon People rather than being introduced from the outside.

Pottery was discovered as far back as the early Jomon Period. In fact, the word Jomon means “rope pattern.” It refers to the unique and characteristic practice the Jomon people had of pressing rope or cord into wet clay before firing it to create a distinct textured appearance. This pottery allowed them to store food, water plants, and cook. It also allowed them to live further away from sources of water such as streams and rivers.

By the late Jomon, they had refined the longbow to a point they could reliably fire arrows up to 50 to 60 meters away. However, due to the lack of stopping power these arrows had, historians believe they tipped their arrows with a poison such as a wolfsbane.

The Jomon People lived in round or rectangular houses with thatched roofs that were partially buried in the earth. These were known as “pit dwellings.” They made use of indoor fireplaces for cooking and warmth.

It is a unique occurrence in history that the Jomon people were able to have such large and permanent dwellings without relying on agriculture. Typically, hunter-gatherers are nomadic people who follow the migration of animals they rely on for food. Scientists believe the fertile soil of

Japan combined with warm, favorable weather conditions meant there was an abundance of nut-bearing trees and other food sources that made agriculture unnecessary.

As the population grew, larger and larger settlements formed. This gave birth to a network of trade between these different settlements. They were able to trade resources such as fish, meat, or certain varieties of edible plants. There was even a large village with over 700 buildings that appears to have been a central trade hub for the different villages. The Jomon Period appears to have been a time of relative peace. The skeletal remains found do not indicate a high incidence of death at the hands of other humans.

By the end of the Jomon Period, the population decreased sharply to only about 76,000. This massive depopulation was likely caused by food shortages. Since Jomon society relied heavily on Japan's abundant natural resources, this also made them susceptible to an adverse change in the climate. It is also likely that the increased population used their resources faster than nature could replenish them. Remember, they weren't farming on any appreciable scale, just taking the bounty of the earth and waiting for nature to give them more. This reduced population set the stage for the next wave of immigrants, the Yayoi.

The Yayoi

The period from 300 BCE and 250 CE is known as the Yayoi period. Between 1,000 and 800 BCE, an ethnically distinct group of people known as the Yayoi migrated from the mainland to the Japanese archipelago. They mixed with the Jomon people to form the ancestors of the modern Japanese people.

One of the hallmarks of the Yayoi period is the shift from hunting and gathering towards agriculture. Compared to

China and Europe, Japan was very late to adopt farming. For context, here are a few things that were happening in the rest of the world at this time. Han Dynasty China was inventing paper, water clocks, and sundials, and the adjustable wrench. During this time, the Greek classical period was just ending. Greece had already advanced in philosophical thought, the art of theater, and a political system known as democracy. By the end of the Yayoi period, the mighty Roman Empire was in decline.

The origins of the Yayoi people are a matter of scholarly debate. Many historians suspect they came to Japan either via the Korean peninsula crossing the Tsushima Strait or from the north of China via the Yellow Sea.

When the Yayoi arrived, they encountered the Jomon people who had already been living on the Japanese archipelago for thousands of years. The Yayoi introduced them to techniques, such as wet-rice farming and metalworking.

One popular legend regarding the origins of the Yayoi people centers around a man named Xu Fu. As the story goes, China's first Emperor and Qin Dynasty founder, Qin Shi Huang, was the target of multiple assassination attempts. After the third attempt on his life, he grew obsessed with the idea of attaining immortality. He summoned his court sorcerer, Xu Fu. The emperor gave Xu Fu the task of finding an elixir of immortality. The emperor instructed Xu Fu to go find the mountain of the immortals where he would meet a thousand-year-old magician that would possess this potion. To this end, the emperor assembled a fleet of ships and recruited a crew of young men seeking adventure and honor.

Xu Fu returned after a few years and claimed that a massive sea monster was obstructing their way. He requested the emperor equip his fleet with archers so they could slay the monster and proceed with their quest. The emperor granted his wish. Xu Fu and his fleet left the harbor, never to return. Legend says Xu Fu landed in Japan because he believed Mount Fuji was the fabled mountain of immortals. He and his men settled there and thus were the Yayoi people. It is improbable that this is more than a mere legend since there are some inconsistencies in matching up the timeline of the Yayoi's arrival in Japan and Xu Fu's voyage. Nevertheless, this tale does point to the importance of China's influence on Japan which we will see play out in the chapters to come.

Regardless of their origins, the Yayoi encountered a Jomon people that were in decline. They were hungry and had stripped the land of its resources. The Yayoi brought the technology of wet rice farming and changed everything. They set up rice paddies which provided a steady and reliable source of food to permanent settlements. This allowed for a massive population boom.

There is some debate among scholars as to whether the Yayoi peacefully assimilated the Jomon people or colonized them (Origins of the Yayoi people, 2008). What is clear is that there was cultural assimilation of Jomon practices such as living in pit dwellings. This indicates a high level of interaction and trade between the two groups.

Armed with their superior technology, the Yayoi population quickly outpaced the Jomon. They produced more simple, functional pottery than the Jomon. They created and popularized bronze bells and mirrors. They also developed spiritual practices that evolved over time into what would be known as the Shinto religion.

A major principle of the Yayoi belief system that would later develop into Shinto is the idea of purity (known as "harae"). Essentially, they posited that humans were born pure and collected impurity over time. Impurities (known as "kegare") included anything relating to death, childbirth, menstruation, and rape. These impurities could be cleansed from someone through rituals such as bathing. Such concepts and rituals persist in Japan to this day.

The growing ubiquity of wet rice farming introduced by the Yayoi meant that people stayed in permanent settlements. During this time, society also stratified into a strict class system. The growing inequality and importance of social class is still felt today in language and customs which aim to show respect from subordinates to their superiors. In Yayoi culture, men were able to have multiple wives. Men of higher status had more wives than those of a lower social class.

The Yayoi did not have a writing system, so much of the information we have today about them comes from archeological evidence and the writings of the Chinese (Prehistory of Japan (Paleolithic, Jōmon and Yayoi periods), n.d.). The Chinese record that during the time of the Yayoi, Japan was broken into 100 kingdoms. There were roughly 30 kingdoms that traded directly with Japan. With the growing inequality of social classes, those at the top amassed greater and greater wealth. This led to war and intense rivalries between the different kingdoms, powered by the newly introduced bronze weapons.

The Yayoi people lived in clans called "uji." The leader of each clan was not only a political leader, but also a religious leader of said clan. Each clan had its own spirit (or god) called a "kami." When one clan conquered another, they also conquered its kami. This meant they grew in spiritual power. Eventually, one state emerged as the dominant force in Japan. This was known as the kingdom of Yamatai. Their ruler was a shaman-queen called Himiko. She partly achieved her power through trade as a tributary kingdom with China.

The influence of China on Japan in this period cannot be overstated. China was well aware of its political dominance throughout Asia. It asserted this power by forcing all kingdoms that traded with China to do so as a subservient, tributary state. These kingdoms would give gifts to China as a tribute to China's greatness. In return, China would give gifts, titles, and honors to these kingdoms. Japanese kingdoms that received this kind of recognition from mighty China gained a certain legitimacy in the region.

The Ainu

To the north, lived another distinctly separate group of people from both the Yayoi and the Jomon People. While they may not have a lasting impact on the Jomon and Yayoi, their culture is unique, fascinating, and certainly deserves to be mentioned here. These people are known as the Ainu.

The Ainu inhabited Japan's northern island, Hokkaido. The majority of the estimated 25,000 remaining Ainu people living today still reside here. The origin of the Ainu people is largely unknown. Some claim they descended from a group of Jomon People who went north, breaking off from the main population and thus maintaining the hunter-gatherer lifestyle of Japan's early settlers. It is also possible that they came to Japan as a completely separate group of people.

The Ainu have a distinct appearance. They have light skin, European-shaped eyes, thick wavy hair, and the men grow full, thick beards. The Ainu women were covered in tattoos. This began as a small black dot on the upper lip. As they

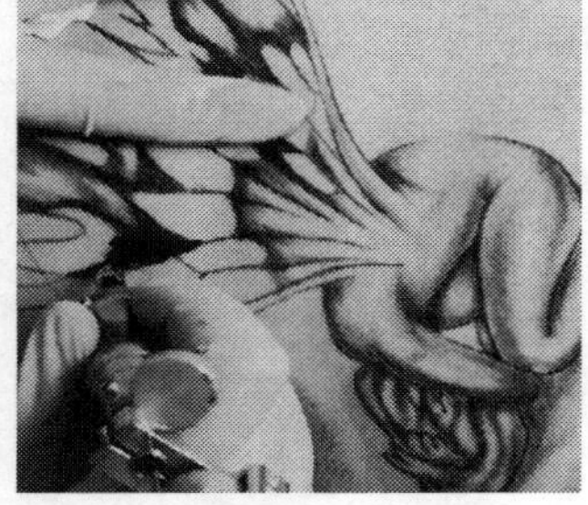

matured, more tattooing was added until a black tattoo surrounded the woman's mouth and eventually her forearms too. These were said to ward off evil spirits. The pain of tattooing was also supposed to prepare the woman for the pain of childbirth. In fact, a fully tattooed woman was a sign that she was of marrying age. Conversely, men never shaved past a certain age. Both men and women kept their hair at roughly shoulder length.

Like the mainland Japanese, the Ainu were animistic, meaning they believed that everything had a spirit (or "kami"). To the Ainu people, the chief amongst these was "Kim-un Kamuy." This was the spirit of bears and the mountains. The bear was believed to be the highest god. The Ainu practiced a tradition known as "lotame," which involved raising a bear from a cub as one of their children. Then, when the bear cub reached adulthood, the Ainu would sacrifice the bear to release the "kamuy."

The Ainu language was (and is) distinct from mainland Japanese. During the Meiji restoration in 1899, the Japanese government began a campaign of forced assimilation of the

Ainu people. They outlawed the Ainu from speaking their native language or participating in their native customs. It was not until 1997 that this ban was lifted, though by this time Ainu culture had been all but wiped out. Today, the remaining Ainu are attempting to preserve their culture and pass it on to the next generations.

空手道

CHAPTER 2
MYTHS

Before moving further down the timeline of historical events, let's take a moment to talk about the colorful myths and legends of Japan. These tales and stories are as much a part of a society as its wars and migrations, perhaps even more so. To truly understand the Japanese people and culture, let's briefly examine some of the most popular myths that help shape the nation. We will, of course, be unable to recount every myth in the massive Japanese canon. We will also be unable to describe all the regional variations on each myth or the ways in which they changed over time. Here we will examine a few foundational myths that will help us to appreciate the culture of this rich and storied nation.

The Japanese Creation Myth

Before there was land, the world was covered by an enormous sea. There were two kami (god or spirit) siblings named Izanagi and Izanami. These names translate literally into "he who invites" and "she who invites," respectively. They received orders from the other kami to solidify the shape of the Earth. Together, they thrust a jeweled spear into the water and churned it. Mud congealed on the tip of the spear. When they lifted the spear from the water, the mud fell into the sea forming an island.

Izanagi and Izanami went down to live on the island. They fell in love and married one another. They had eight children, which became the eight main islands of Japan. They gave birth to many more kami after that, such as the Kamis of wind, mountains, and rivers. When Izanami gave birth to the kami of fire, however, she was badly burned. Izanagi knelt beside his dying wife/sister in tears. As his tears fell, each tear created a new kami.

Izanami died and was sent to the underworld. In his grief, Izanagi went to the underworld to find her. Izanami told him that she would ask the kami of the underworld to release her but warned Izanagi not to look at her. After a time, curiosity got the better of Izanagi. He lit a torch so he could see his beloved Izanami once more. He was horrified to see that she was now a hideous, rotting corpse. In terror, he ran. Izanami chased him.

When Izanagi returned to the land of the living, he placed a giant boulder in front of the entrance to the underworld. From behind the boulder, Izanami yelled that she would kill 1,000 people every day if he left her. Izanagi replied that in that case, he could create 1,500 people every day. This explained why every day many people die and still more people are born.

Izanagi took a bath to purify himself. When Izanagi washed his left eye, the kami of the sun, Amaterasu, was created. When he washed his right eye, the kami of the moon, Tsukiyomi, was created. When he washed his nose, the kami of storms and the sea, Susanoo, was created. Amaterasu became the most important kami. All emperors of Japan claim to be descendants of this sun goddess.

Amaterasu

Amaterasu is the powerful kami of the sun and one of the most important kami in Japanese mythology. As such, there are many myths about her. This is one of the most popular and enduring.

Disappearance of the Sun

Susanoo, the kami of the seas, was neglecting his duties and cried about how he longed to see his mother, Izanami, in the underworld. So, his father, Izanagi, sent him to go live in the underworld. Prior to leaving, Susanoo decided to visit his sister, Amaterasu, to say goodbye. She knew of Susanoo's reputation as a troublemaker, so when she heard Susanoo was coming, she armed herself for battle. Susanoo was insulted that his sister did not trust him and they got into a big disagreement. To settle the argument, he challenged her to a contest. Amaterasu agreed.

Amaterasu asked for Susanoo's sword. She then broke it into three pieces. Then she chewed them up and spat them out, creating three new kami. Susanoo then asked Amaterasu for her jewels. He chewed them up and spit out five new kami. Susanoo won the contest.

Susanoo then began to gloat over his victory. In his raucous celebration, he destroyed farmland and property. He flayed a horse and threw it at Amaterasu's loom, inadvertently killing one of her maidens.

At this insult, Amaterasu went into a cave and shut herself in with a boulder. With the kami of the sun gone, the earth was plunged into darkness. Chaos ensued. The rest of the kami convened to see what they could do to convince Amaterasu to come out of the cave. They brought forth a large mirror. The kami Ame no Uzume, The Great Persuader, danced naked before a cheering crowd.

Amaterasu peeked out from the cave to see why everyone was cheering and celebrating. Ame no Uzume told her an even better and more beautiful kami than Amaterasu had come. They held up the mirror, showing Amaterasu her reflection. Amaterasu pushed the boulder back further to get a better look when one of the kami pulled Amaterasu out from the cave. Another kami pushed the boulder back over the opening to the cave and sealed it shut with a sacred rope called "shimenawa," so she could not go back in.

Now that Amaterasu and her light returned to the world once again, the other kami approached Susanoo. As punishment for his behavior, they required him to provide 1,000 tables full of offerings to them. They shaved his beard, removed his nails, and cast him out of heaven.

The Fabled Sword Kusanagi

At the coronation of each Japanese Emperor, they are presented with three items that serve as proof of the Emperor's divinity. These items are known as the Imperial Regalia. They consist of the jewel Yasakani no Magatama from the contest between Amaterasu and Susanoo mentioned above, the mirror Yata no Kagami that was used to lure Amaterasu from her cave in the previous myth, and the sword Kusanagi no Tsurugi.

This is the tale of how the kami Susanoo came to possess the sword Kusanagi.

Having been banished from heaven, Susanoo was walking beside a river when he came across two parents and their daughter who were all weeping. Susanoo asked them what was wrong. The parents told him that they had eight daughters, but every year a horrible serpent monster with eight heads, Yamata no Orochi, killed and ate one of their daughters. Now they had only one daughter left. They were crying because it was almost time for the serpent to arrive again and they feared they would lose their last remaining daughter.

Susanoo offered to slay the serpent in exchange for their daughter's hand in marriage. The family agreed. Susanoo turned the daughter into a comb. He puts the comb in his hair to keep the daughter safe and close by. Susanoo then instructed the old couple to fill eight vats with sake and place them behind a fence with eight gates, one behind each gate. The couple did as they were told.

When the serpent appeared, it fell for Susanoo's trap and placed one head in each vat of sake to drink from it. Susanoo acted quickly, slicing off each of the eight heads one by one. Then he began to hack off the creature's tails as well. When he tried to slice off the forth tail, his sword broke. He discovered that inside this tail, there was an exquisite sword. He named the sword Ame-no-Murakumo-no-Tsurugi ("Heavenly Sword of Gathering Clouds). He presented this sword to Amaterasu to help make amends for his previous behavior towards her.

Many years later, under the reign of Emperor Keikō, the sword was given to Yamato Takeru, a great and powerful warrior. Takeru was lured into a grass field. His enemy used flaming arrows to set fire to the field, trapping Takeru, so he would die in the flames. Takeru used the sword to cut down the grass, so the fire could not spread. He discovered that the sword also had a magical ability to control the wind. He was able to use it to redirect the fire towards his enemies and win the battle. After this victory, Takeru renamed the sword Kusanagi-no-Tsurugi ("Grass Cutting Sword").

CHAPTER 3
NARA AND HEIAN PERIODS

Nara Period

The Nara period lasted from 710 to 794 CE. This was the time when Japan's capital was in Heijo-kyo, or present-day Nara. This would become Japan's first permanent capital city. Prior to this, a new capital was built for each Japanese Emperor. This was likely due to the concept of impurity we mentioned in the previous chapter. The death of the Emperor made the old capital impure, therefore a new one needed to be built.

The capital at Nara was modeled after the Chinese capital and was the most lavish capital Japan had had thus far. The capital was moved a few times during the Nara period. In 740, Emperor Shōmu moved the capital to Kuni-kyo. In 743, it was moved to Shiragaki-kyo. Then in 745, the capital was moved back to Nara. Here it remained, until 784 when it was moved to Nagaoka-kyo. Then it was moved to Heian-kyo (modern day Kyoto) in 794.

The Nara period was the period in which the Fujiwara clan

began their rise to power by marrying their daughters to Emperors and high-ranking officials in the Imperial Court. In 645 CE, Prince Nakano Ōe (later known as Emperor Tenji) had led a coup against the powerful Soga clan and seized power for himself. Nakatomi Kamatari had assisted him in this coup. For his support, Emperor Tenji gave Nakatomi Kamatari the name Fujiwara.

A series of government reforms followed this coup that was known as the Taika No Kaishin, or Taika era reforms. As Japan moved towards a more powerful centralized government, a series of laws were put in place that made the position of the Emperor more and more influential.

During the Nara period, the Japanese also began writing. While there had been some writing during the prior Asuka period, it did not become widespread until the Nara period. It was in this period that the Nihon Shoki and Kojiki were written. These were a blend of history and myth that told the origin stories of Japan, Shinto legends, and solidified the legitimacy of the Japanese Emperors by claiming their direct descendants from the sun goddess, Amaterasu. The Nihon Shoki was written in Chinese, whereas the Kojiki was written in a blend of Chinese characters and unique Japanese characters.

This increase in writing would set the stage for an explosion of writing and innovation in the Heian Period that followed.

Heian Period

Following the political reforms of the Nara Period, the Heian Period marks the era in which Japan's capital stayed in Heian-kyo (modern-day Kyoto). This period lasted from 794-1185 CE. While scholars disagree as to why exactly the capital was moved from Nara to Heian-kyo, a common theory posits that Emperor Kanmu wished to escape the political might of the Buddhist temples (The Heian Period, an Age of Art... Ending in a Shogunate | History of Japan 34, n.d.).

Why the Capital Moved to Heian-kyo

In the late Nara Period, the retired Empress Kōken had fallen ill. She called for an ascetic monk by the name of Dōkyō. He claimed to have magical powers gained through his Buddhist spiritual practices which he used to cure the Empress. The Empress was grateful to Dōkyō and rewarded him by giving him titles and political power. There were rumors that the Empress even took Dōkyō as a lover. When the former Empress stripped Emperor Junnin of his rank and exiled him, she promoted Dōkyō to the position of daijō-daijin which gave him authority over religious and civil affairs. The Empress also instituted a new law that would allow her to pick her successor. Many assumed she would select Dōkyō. Since he did not have royal blood, this would end the old line of emperors and start a new line. There were also fears he would create a theocracy, giving Buddhists political control over Japan.

Dōkyō promoted members of his relatively unknown and unprestigious clan to high-ranking government positions, including his brother. He limited the amount of land that nobles could own but set no such restrictions on Buddhist Temples.

The current nobles were understandably less than pleased with Dōkyō's rise to power, especially as it meant losing their own power. These tensions came to a head when an oracle delivered the prophecy that if Dōkyō were made Emperor, it would bring peace to the country. This enraged the nobles, particularly the Fujiwara clan. It was seen as confirmation of a coup by a lesser clan that would strip them of their power.

Shortly thereafter, in 770 CE, the Empress died. She had been Dōkyō's main champion. With her out of the picture, the Fujiwara clan moved quickly to strip Dōkyō of his rank and exile him. Dōkyō would die in relative obscurity.

It is likely the capital was moved to distance the Imperial court from a large number of Buddhist shrines in Nara. It is also possible that this incident, known as the Dōkyō Incident, was responsible for the lack of any female Emperors for the next 1,000 years.

Politics of Heian Japan

At the start of the Heian Period, the Emperor had more power than ever before. Japan was much more unified than in the prior periods we've discussed. As always, Japan looked toward China for inspiration. The Chinese Emperor strove to be an absolute ruler (remember when we spoke in the previous chapter about the system of tributary trade China instituted). Early Heian emperors strove to attain this ideal.

However, in Japan, the political climate was different. People felt more loyalty to their clan than to the emperor. Thus, the top clans continually jockeyed for more political control. China used a civil service exam for government positions, meaning those who had proven their competence got promoted to higher ranks. In Japan, high-ranking positions were given based on clan loyalty and who they married.

In 781 CE, Kanmu was named emperor—the first of the Heian Period. In terms of his actual political authority, he was said to be the most powerful emperor in Japanese history. The Fujiwara clan had been the greatest threat to the authority of the emperor. But when Kanmu took the throne in 781 CE, there were no strong representatives of the clan in the imperial court.

Much of northern Japan was still not under Japanese imperial rule. Kanmu consequently sent armies to attack what were seen as the barbarian tribes that lived there. He also moved the capital twice: from Nara to Nagaoka-kyo, then to Heian-kyo. There was also a practice of giving shoen (tax-free, private land) to nobles as gifts, meaning there was less land being taxed. The combined effect of these changes was a massive drain on the government's financial resources.

To increase cash flow to the imperial coffers, Kanmu began to increase taxes on the provinces. He also set up two new important bureaus. The first was called the Kurodo-dokoro, which handled imperial documents. The other was called the Kebiishii, which was the Emperor's police force. The Kebiishii had the power to arrest, judge, and punish criminals (including tax evaders). These new bureaus consolidated power and allowed the emperor to eliminate half of the previous government offices. This also saved the government money.

Kanmu also began limiting the number of descendants that were considered a part of the imperial house. These royal family members were costly, as they were given riches, homes, and luxuries befitting of their station. Kanmu limited who was considered a member of the royal family. He limited this class to the fourth generation from the emperor. At the time he implemented this, it meant over 100 existing members of the imperial house were demoted. He also reduced the amount of money given to royal family members. Many of the demoted members left the capital and headed for the provinces. This inadvertently increased the political power of the provincial governments.

Due to a lack of funds, the imperial court also began paying court officials in land. Since this land could be used by the officials to make their own money, they became less reliant on the imperial court. The Emperor also claimed large tracts of land for himself, meaning there was even less taxable land.

All of these factors meant less power for the emperor and more power for the clans. Specifically, the Fujiwara clan. Since the clan had assisted Emperor Tenji to come to power back in the Nara Period, they had been able to leverage this to amass great power. This included a law that said Emperors had to marry either a Fujiwara or from the imperial family. Also, only Fujiwara men could marry the daughters of emperors. In 857, Fujiwara no Yoshifusa was named chancellor, which was the highest office besides emperor in the Japanese government.

The following year, Yoshifusa's son was named Emperor Seiwa. He was just nine years old at the time, making him Japan's first child emperor. He was also the first emperor to be controlled by a regent. Previously, the mothers of child emperors would take the throne until their son came of age, keeping the power in the hands of the royal family. The regent held the power of the emperor without having to be a member of the imperial family.

Then in 866 CE, one of the gates of the imperial palace burned down. It's unclear what the true cause of the fire was, but a court investigation placed the blame on the Otomo and Ki clans. These clans had held power in the imperial courts for generations and were some of the biggest obstacles to the Fujiwara dominance. By ousting them, the Fujiwara clan was able to step in and seize even more political control.

Now the Otomo and Ki clans were gone, Fujiwara no

Yoshifusa had little trouble stepping into the role of regent. Yoshifusa's son, Fujiwara no Motosone, also became regent. In 884 CE, an adult emperor named Kōkō ascended. Since a regent could only rule for a child emperor, Motosone created the position of Kanpaku (regent for an adult emperor).

The office of Kanpaku became a permanent position that would remain in the control of the Fujiwara clan. This allowed them to maintain a stranglehold on the government for the next 200 years. At this point, the emperor of Japan lost all real political authority.

The upper classes had reached the pinnacle of what we might consider the "idle rich." This was an era when increasingly elaborate rituals became central to court life. The era came to be known for the "cult of beauty." It was fashionable for the upper classes to bemoan how fleeting all that is beautiful. This was likely influenced by the Buddhist idea that attachment to worldly things is the root of all suffering. However, suffering was also seen as quite fashionable.

Art and Romance

Another distinguishing feature of the Heian Courts was what would be considered today as rampant cheating. There was a huge divide, of course, between the lives of upper-class aristocrats and the peasants of the provinces. Since surviving art and literature were generally created by the upper classes for the upper classes, it's this small section of society we have the clearest understanding of—it was fascinating.

In the Heian era, court ladies had more freedom than in previous eras, yet they could not leave their homes, except on special occasions such as festivals or to visit temples. Women at this time were paradoxically considered inferior to men and, at the same time, more valuable than men. The teachings of the Chinese philosopher Confucius emphasized that women were inferior. Buddhist teachings claimed that a woman had to be reincarnated as a man before they could attain enlightenment. Women could not take part in government. However, inheritance of property generally went to women, violence against women was prohibited, and, due to marriage politics, women were able to climb the social ladder through marriage more easily than men.

Women mostly remained in their private quarters, greeting visitors only when hidden behind screens. Most of their communication was done via exchanging notes, which contained poetry. Being able to compose beautiful poems on the spot was an important skill that was expected of all nobles of this time period.

Noblewomen were also not allowed to do their own housework, or even to raise their own children. Much of their lives consisted of idle time and boredom. Common hobbies of the time included practicing arts, such as music and calligraphy. The board game Go was also a popular pastime.

Another common pastime for Heian women was writing.

While men of the era were expected to learn Chinese and write for practical, business-related purposes, women were free to experiment. It was at this time that the new Japanese script Hiragana, meaning simple script (simple as opposed to Chinese characters known as kanji). Interestingly, famous authors of this era were almost all women.

This was the time in which Sei Shōnagon wrote her famous collection of musings on courtly life known as The Pillow Book. Another author named Murasaki Shikibu wrote a book that is widely considered to be the first modern novel, The Tale of Genji. Shikibu's story was among the first to focus on the inner emotional lives of its characters rather than place focus on a recitation of events. The book tells the story of Genji, a fictional son of a fictional emperor, and the tragedies of his many romantic conquests.

Though fictional, The Tale of Genji provides insight into the intrigue of court life. Cheating was an open secret amongst the upper class. A man was expected to take many lovers. Women were supposed to remain faithful to their men, however, in practice, this just meant to not get caught cheating.

There were no strong religious ideas about sex being sinful, like in Judeo-Christian traditions. There was a custom that men would exchange letters and poems with the woman he desired. If she showed interest in return, he would sneak into her house and attempt to woo and seduce her. A man of the high station was expected to have many mistresses. Marriages past the first marriage were not an official legal process either. If a man continued to see a woman, they could be said to be married. If he stopped seeing her, that could be considered a divorce. But if he came back later, he may say that he never divorced her. So relationships could get a bit complicated.

Women of the Heian era also had a very distinct sense of fashion. They wore stark white makeup, drew their eyebrows high on their forehead, and stained their teeth black. They wore layers of robes in a style known as ni-hito (literally meaning "12 layers"), though some women wore as many as 40 layers depending on their status and the occasion.

The Genpei War

This quiet, peaceful time of poetry appreciation couldn't last forever, though. In fact, it ended with a bloody civil war that began the era of samurai rule in Japan. This civil war was known as the Genpei War.

The major players in the conflict were the Taira and Minamoto, clans. The two clans had been vying for control of the Imperial court for decades. During the Hōgen and Heiji Rebellions, the Minamoto clan attempted to take control of the Taira clan but were unsuccessful.

In 1180, Emperor Takakura abdicated. Taira no Kiyomori put his two-year-old grandson on the throne. Mochihito, the son of Emperor Go-Shirakawa, was furious. He felt he had been denied his right to the throne. Jumping at the chance to take down the Taira, Minamoto no Yorimasa mobilized the Minamoto clan and sought help from Buddhist monasteries.

Kiyomori called for Mochihito's arrest. The Taira chased Mochihito to Byōdō-in, just outside the capital. The forces met at the bridge over the river Uji in the first dramatic battle of the war. The Taira overpowered the Minamoto forces. Yorimasa committed seppuku, an honorable suicide of the feudal Japanese samurai class, and Mochihito was executed.

Enraged by their loss, Minamoto's new leader, Minamoto no Yoritomo, began calling for allied clans to join his side and fight the Taira. On his travels, Yoritomo and his forces were repelled by the Taira at Hakone Pass. The Minamoto found supporters in the provinces of Kōzuke and Kai who helped them to fend off the Taira.

Then in 1181 CE, Taira no Kiyomori died of fever. A famine followed and the fighting stopped for two years. When the fighting resumed with the Battle of Kurikara in 1183, the Taira suffered a devastating defeat. The Minamoto forced the Taira army to flee the capital.

The years following saw the Taira fighting vainly to reassert their control and find a foothold. At last, in 1185 CE, the war culminated in a great sea battle called the Battle of Dan-no-ura. The Minamoto defeated the Taira and brought an end to Taira dominance in the Imperial courts once and for all. Emperor Go-Shirakawa gave Minamoto no Yoritomo the power to collect taxes and appoint jito (stewards) and shugo (constables) in all of the provinces. This meant the emperor had just handed over all real political power to a military leader. When Emperor Go-Shirakawa died in 1192 CE, Yoritomo was given the title of Sei-i Tai Shōgun (literally "barbarian-subduing great general"). The seat of the shogunate, Kamakura, was now the effective capital. Kyoto was relegated to a place of ceremony and ritual.

The age of the samurai was about to begin.

CHAPTER 4
KAMAKURA PERIOD

The Kamakura Period lasted from the end of the Genpei War in 1185 CE until the violent end of the Kamakura shogunate in 1333 CE. It was the time in which the samurai came to power and feudalism was established in Japan.

Minamoto no Yoritomo, now the leader of the new military government, set to work murdering his potential rivals—starting with his brother Yoshitsune. He went on to kill his nephew, the son Yoshitsune had by a concubine. He also killed another one of his brothers, Noriyori, and his daughter's fiance.

While Yoritomo's new shogunate in Kamakura held all the military power, he still made sure to get official authorization from the Kyoto government for all his policies. When Yoritomo died in 1199, the title of shogun passed to his son, Yoriie.

Yoritomo's wife, Hojo Masako, had strong loyalty to the Hojo clan, which was a small part of the larger Taira clan. Her father was Hojo Tokimasa, head of the Hojo family and lord of some lands in the Izu province. There is an interesting story surrounding the way Masako and Yoritomo met. After his father had been defeated by the Taira during the Heiji Rebellion, Yoritomo had been banished to the Izu province. During his exile, Masako's sister caught his eye. So he wrote a letter and asked a samurai to deliver it to her. But the samurai delivered the letter to Masako by mistake. Her father, Tokimasa, understandably disapproved of his daughter marrying a Minamoto and forbade Masako from marrying him. In defiance, Masako ran away from home in the night, embarking on a long mountain trek to be with Yoritomo. The two lived in hiding in a mountain temple until Tokimasa at last relented and allowed them to marry.

The Hojo did not want Yoriie to be shogun. The Hojo placed Yoriie under house arrest for plotting against the Hojo. Yoriie was assassinated by the clan a year later. The title of shogun then passed to his younger brother, Sanetomo. He was just a child at the time, meaning he would need a regent to rule for him. This made the shogun a mere figurehead, while the Hojo regents held all the real power—an arrangement that would last through the end of the Kamakura Period.

After Yoritomo's death, Hojo Masako became a nun. But despite her religious vows, she went about amassing more political power. Thus, she would be known as the Nun Shogun.

Jokyu War

Retired Emperor Gotoba feared the growing power of the new military government in Kamakura. He wanted to bring power back to the emperor and the traditional government in Kyoto. So in 1221 CE, he set in motion a chain of events that led to the embarrassing Jokyu war.

Gotoba assembled an army consisting of the Taira and other enemies of the Minamoto clan from the earlier Genpei War. Gotoba decided on the lines of succession for the throne without running it by the Kamakura government. He then held a festival, inviting all of his potential allies. He assumed those who refused were loyal to the Kamakura government over his Kyoto government. Gotoba even had one officer killed for exposing his loyalty to the shogunate.

A few days later, Gotoba declared the shogunate's regent, Hōjō Yoshitoki, to be an outlaw. The shogunate retaliated to this declaration by mobilizing their own army and heading for Kyoto. The Kamakura armies smashed their way through Gotoba's forces. Gotoba fled the city, seeking protection from the warrior monks of Mount Hiei. However, the monks could see the writing on the wall and refused to back the loser of this conflict. Gotoba's forces made one last stand at the bridge over the river Uji, the same site where the Genpei War began. The shogun army made short work of them and took the city of Kyoto for themselves. Gotoba and his sons were banished to the Oki Islands, never to return.

The Kamakura government began taking land from members of the losing side. The military government's power grew far greater than that of the traditional government.

First Mongol Invasion

The next major battle would come as a threat from the mainland. The Mongols under the leadership of Kublai Khan had just made the Korean kingdom of Goryeo into a vassal state and were feeling optimistic about their chances of continued conquests. In 1266 CE and 1267 CE respectively, the Mongols had sent emissaries to Japan demanding they send tribute and agree to become a vassal state as well. Both times, Japan refused. Over the following years, the Mongols continued to send similar demands, but by this point, Japan wasn't even allowing the Mongol emissaries' ships to land.

The traditional Kyoto government thought it would be wise to try and negotiate with the Mongols rather than risk starting a war. But after the Shogunate had slapped all respect out of the

Kyoto government in the Jokyu War, Kyoto's appeals fell on deaf ears. Instead, the proud Shogunate ordered all the landholders in Kyūshū, the province where the Mongols were most likely to attack, to return to their lands and prepare for battle.

In 1274 CE, the Mongols left the Korean Peninsula and landed on the Japanese island of Tsushima. The *jitodai* (deputy governor) along with his tiny force of 80 samurai rode out to meet the invading Mongol force of 8,000 warriors on 900 ships. The jitodai attempted to negotiate, but the Mongols promptly shot him dead with arrows and killed the 80 samurai. The Mongol forces then took the island of Iki with similar ease, defeating a resistance of 100 samurai. The Mongols allegedly hung the naked bodies of the women they murdered from the sides of their ships.

The Mongols reached Hakata Bay on November 19th. The Japanese defenders equaled them in number, but the Mongol battle tactics took the Japanese by surprise. The Mongols formed a phalanx using shields and poleaxes. They came equipped with bombs that spooked the Japanese horses and terrified the men.

The battle lasted a day and a half. The Mongol forces killed one-third of the Japanese defenders, forced them to retreat to Mizuki castle, and burned Hakata to the ground. The Japanese forces regrouped at Mizuki castle and made ready for a last stand against the terrifying invaders. But no such attack came. Legend says that a sudden typhoon arose that forced the Mongol ships away from the island.

Second Mongol Invasion

After the first invasion, the shogunate correctly guessed that the Mongols would try to invade again and began preparing for just such an event. In the years that followed, they constructed forts and walls at likely landing spots.

Kublai Khan sent even more emissaries to Japan to demand once again that Japan agree to become a vassal state and send tributes. This time they refused to leave without a response. So the Japanese cut their heads off and sent those back to Kublai Khan as a response.

The Mongols had just conquered the Song dynasty in China, meaning they had extra manpower for this second invasion. Kublai Khan wasn't messing around this time, even using death row prisoners to bolster the size of his army. By the time he launched his attack in 1281 CE, he had 900 ships from Korea and 1,500 ships from southern China set to demolish all Japanese resistance.

This time, Kublai Khan had decided on a two-pronged attack strategy. A portion of the Mongol forces attacked from an Eastern Route heading again for the island of Tsushima then to Iki. They were supposed to wait for the Southern Route forces at Iki, but the commanders ignored their orders and went off to attack the Japanese mainland all by themselves. Not only that, but the Eastern fleet weakened themselves even further by splitting up Scooby-Doo style to invade both the Nagato Province and Hakata Bay simultaneously. The Japanese at Nagato pushed the Mongol forces back to Iki.

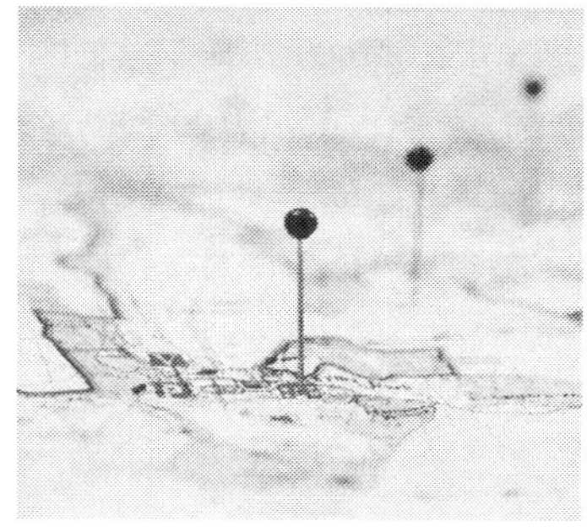

The forces that landed at Hakata Bay could not make it through all the fortifications the Japanese had put in place. The Mongols retreated to the islands of Noko and Shika with the Japanese launching a series of counter-attacks against them the whole while.

When the Southern fleet was finally able to meet up with the Eastern fleet, they tried to use their combined forces to Hakata, but again the Japanese held strong. Unable to land, the invading Mongol forces dropped anchor and fastened their ships together. Then, a powerful typhoon arose and completely demolished the invaders' ships. This typhoon would go down in history as *kamikaze* or divine wind. Even retreating ships were not spared. Mongol forces were seen in the water, clinging to pieces of their broken ships. When they washed ashore, they were executed by the Japanese. The Chinese, however, were spared since the Japanese felt they had only taken part in the attacks due to Kublai Khan's coercion.

Aftermath of the Invasion

While Japan's victory against the Mongol army was impressive, it caused some serious issues for the Kamakura government. Since this was a defensive war, Japan had acquired no new land. The government was running short on land to pay the samurai who fought off the invasion. Also, the Buddhist monks who had performed rituals and ceremonies to ward off the invaders were also demanding payment—declaring that their work had brought the *kamikaze.* Having fought valiantly and received little to no reward, dissent began to spread amongst the samurai class. Loyalty to the Kamakura government began to weaken.

As the samurai divided their land to give to their children, each successive generation had less land and resources than the previous one. The Shogunate was aware of this growing unrest. To try to help the situation, the Kamakura government declared that samurai's land could only be passed down to one male heir. In the Heian era, land had been passed down to daughters which had given women more power. While mothers could pass on land to their daughters under this new policy, the number of landowning women began to taper off dramatically.

Another factor chipping away at women's rights in this era was the spread of Buddhism. The type of Buddhism that entered Japan had come through China. This meant it picked up Confucian ideas like the impurity of women. While Buddhism had existed in Japan during the Heian Period, it had then been practiced primarily by the upper classes. Now, in the Kamakura Period, Buddhism became prevalent in the provinces and amongst the commoners.

The three most common types of Buddhism in Japan at this time were Pure Land, Nichiren, and Zen Buddhism. Pure Land Buddhism appealed to commoners as it promised a way to reach the Pure Land, a type of Buddhist paradise. This sect centered around the worship of the Amida Buddha, such as repeating his name. Nichiren Buddhism, named for the priest who founded the sect, taught that enlightenment could be attained by reciting the Lotus Sutra. Finally, Zen Buddhism focused on knowing the true self by quieting the mind and acting spontaneously at the moment. The Zen sect was popular amongst the samurai class.

The kamakura period came to an end in 1333 ce under emperor go-daigo as the result of a civil war called the genkō incident. Go-daigo had been plotting to overthrow the kamakura government, but they discovered his plans. The shogunate exiled go-daigo to oki in 1331 (the same place gotoba had been exiled). However, go-daigo was able to escape. General ashikaga takauji had been sent to defeat go-daigo and his men, but again the samurai class was becoming less and less loyal to the kamakura government. Takauji sided with go-daigo and together they overtook kamakura. Hōjō takatoki and his entire family committed seppuku, ending the hōjō clan's reign.

CHAPTER 5

MUROMACHI PERIOD

The Muromachi Period, otherwise known as the Ashikaga Period, lasted from roughly 1333 - 1573 CE. Different sources will cite slightly different start and end dates to this period as we will see. For example, 1333 CE marks the date when the Kamakura government was overthrown in the Genkō Incident. Emperor Go-Daigo had begun this rebellion to bring power back to the Imperial court. After 148 years of military rule, Go-Daigo was thrilled by the success of his revolution. He immediately instituted the Kenmu Restoration, a move to completely restore the imperial court to its former glory. He failed, however, to secure the support of the samurai, such as the very ones who had helped him overthrow the Kamakura government in the first place. So in practice, the Kenmu Restoration amounted to little more than Go-Daigo's fantasy wish-fulfillment that was over almost before it started.

Ashikaga Takauji, the general who had defected from the Kamakura Shogunate to help Go-Daigo overthrow them, became the shogun himself. He established a new shogunate in 1336 CE. This new military government was set up in Ashikaga, just outside of Kyoto, and was thus called the Ashikaga Shogunate. Whereas the Kamakura Shogunate had operated alongside the traditional imperial court, the new Ashikaga Shogunate claimed all the authoritarian power for itself.

The time from 1336-1392 CE was known as the *Nanboku-chō* or Era of the Southern and Northern Courts. Whereas the Northern Court referred to the imperial court of the Ashikaga Shogunate, the Southern Court referred to the traditional imperial court of Go-Daigo. While it was clear that the military might rest with the Northern Court, the Emperor and his Southern Court were not entirely irrelevant. After all, the Emperor had the Imperial Regalia (otherwise known as the Three Treasures), which we discussed in Chapter 2: Mythology. These artifacts are a reminder of the divine authority of the emperor and how the spiritual significance of these tales was still firmly embedded in the nation's identity. It's easy to overlook the spiritual significance of this when viewed through a modern, scientific-materialist lens, but the traditional imperial government was still an influential entity.

The Samurai

While we mentioned Japan's legendary warrior class in the previous chapter, the influence of the samurai would continue to grow and shape Japan. The samurai would leave a legacy that endures to this day. Much has been made of *Bushido,* the samurai code of conduct, and some of the most famous samurai conquests in Japanese history. Let's take a moment to examine just who the samurai were and how they came to leave their mark on the nation's history.

Prior to 792 CE, Japan had a national military. This was not a standing army, but rather a militia. Militiamen lived their normal lives as farmers until some threat to Japan occurred, and they were called to take up arms and defend the country. This was cheaper than maintaining a standing army because they were only used if they were needed. Any able-bodied men between the ages of 20 and 59 could be drafted as needed. In practice, each man served one month per year on average. Since they served so infrequently, they were not highly trained. Nobles from wealthy families that had access to horses and military training might become horseback archers.

In 792 CE, Emperor Kanmu ended the national military. The threat of Chinese invaders was slim since they were embroiled in their own conflicts elsewhere. And there were problems with the existing military model of Japan. There was little loyalty amongst the troops. People dodged the draft or deserted frequently. Governors were using the militia for non-military purposes, such as farming and other projects at the imperial government's expense.

The government started to place more emphasis on those with military training, such as the aforementioned horse archers. They created new titles and took to paying these specialized soldiers for hire whenever the need arose. So it was that in the 800s, a new class of warriors emerged in Japan.

Since social status and rank were closely tied to family lines, there were few opportunities for social mobility for those born outside of a high-ranking clan. The warrior class was appealing to those who had the means to acquire horses and armor but lacked the family name needed to ascend to the upper echelons of the imperial court. Now, however, the opportunity emerged to ascend the social ladder through heroism in battle. Titles, land, and favors were awarded to distinguished warriors. This new class or warrior was known as *bushi* or *samurai* (literally "one who serves").

There were many opportunities for samurai to sell their services. Since more and more people owned private lands, there was a greater need to hire people to protect that land. They could also find work assisting in tax collection, fighting bandits, and quashing rebellions. They could be hired as bodyguards for nobles or even as police in cities.

Some samurai saw the benefit of banding together and forming gangs. The leaders, or warlords, were able to attract new members through promises of riches and other personal gains. These gangs could also form alliances with one another when it was mutually beneficial. This was the path that both the Taira and Minamoto clans we mentioned in the previous chapter used to advance their power and influence. They amassed armies in the provinces and sought favor by taking positions supporting high-ranking nobles in the capital.

While it seems that the growing military power of the warrior class could have posed a threat to imperial power, that wasn't the case—at first. During the Heian Period, samurai groups competed for the titles and acknowledgment of the more powerful clans of the imperial court. If a samurai acted against the ruling class, the court would label it as an act of treason. They would then bestow titles and power upon other samurai and send them to kill the offender, as in the case of Taira no Masakado attacking a provincial headquarters.

As we saw earlier, this all changed at the end of the Heian Period and the beginning of the Kamakura Period when the Minamoto clan rose to power during the Genpei War and established the Kamakura Shogunate. Now in the Muromachi Period, a new Muromachi Shogunate also made use of the samurai class. So in this period, we see a continued increase in the importance of the warrior class.

It's important to understand that the samurai were not loyal to some fuzzy idea of the Japanese state. Rather, they fought for personal gain. Their loyalty was to their clans and to their warlords. One way samurai were incentivized to be brave in battle was through the practice of head taking.

Head Taking

The practice of removing and displaying the heads of one's enemies has ancient roots. It can be traced back at least as far as 200 BCE in China. Like much of Japanese culture, head taking was probably also imported from China. The earliest confirmed reports of head taking in Japan date back to the 900s CE. Though it cannot be confirmed, it is certainly plausible this could have begun even earlier.

The title of samurai was seen (usually) as an honorable position. In battle, it was common for one samurai to single out another on the battlefield and fight one-on-one. The victor would cut off the head of the loser, then present it to his lord for payment. This was a way for the samurai to prove their service in battle. Through this system, a samurai who had collected many heads would gain prestige and honor. In turn, taking the head of such a samurai would also bestow great honor.

One famous early example of head taking in Japan is the tale of Taira no Masakado. He was a Heian-era samurai who led a small rebellion in 939 CE in the provinces, capturing the local governor. In response, the imperial government in Kyoto put a price on Masakado's head. Roughly two months later in 940 CE, he was killed in battle. His head was brought back to Kyoto where it was displayed for the imperial court. The head was later brought to a small fishing village that would later become known as Tokyo. Masakado's head was buried there in a *kubizuka*, a type of grave. Masakado's head became deified and locals began to pay their respects at his *kubizuka*. At times, when his *kubizuka* was neglected, natural disasters seemed to befall Japan. Accordingly, his *kubizuka* is kept well maintained to this day. It is located in Tokyo's financial district on some of the most expensive real estate worldwide.

Prior to the Genpei War and the start of the Kamakura Shogunate, lords lacked the ability to promote samurai to higher social status and give them land to rule. After the war, the military-ruled the country, and *shugo* (military governors) had the power to give land and titles to the samurai. And the quickest way to advance in this new era of social mobility for the warrior class was to present to their lords the heads of the most prestigious enemy samurai they could acquire. The act of presenting these taken heads became a ceremony in itself, known as the “head viewing ceremony.” It’s important to note that even peasants could participate in these ceremonies. So if a feudal serf managed to collect the head of an enemy samurai and present it during a head viewing ceremony, he could be elevated to the status of samurai himself.

During a head viewing ceremony, heads had to be presented in an elegant and respectful manner. As such, a samurai preparing for battle would ensure his own head was presentable in case it should be cut off that day. However, it was ultimately the responsibility of the samurai to take the head to ensure the presentability of whatever heads he acquired. They would wash the head, comb its hair, and blacken its teeth to indicate its noble status. They would then wrap the head in a white cloth and place it on a wooden display, bearing the name of the samurai the head once belonged to as well as who took it.

There were, of course, some issues with this system. Some samurai would try to pass off a lowly footsoldier’s head like that of a high-ranking samurai in order to receive a greater reward. Also, some samurai would leave the battlefield after they had collected an especially valuable head to ensure they got their reward before they were killed (one could say they were quitting while they were *ahead*). Also, removing heads could take a long time. In the heat of battle, when swiftness could mean the difference between victory and defeat, samurai would stop after each kill to see through the necks of each of their fallen foes. Even for all these drawbacks, the practice of head taking would continue in Japan up until WWII.

Samurai Swords

The image of the samurai is all but inseparable from their most iconic weapon—the sword. It is therefore important to take a look into the development and impact of the samurai sword in warrior culture and Japanese culture as a whole.

The *chokuto* (meaning "straight sword") or *tsurugi* was the earliest type of sword produced in Japan. These swords were roughly two feet long and were worn from the warrior's waist. This type of sword existed before the samurai. The technology to produce this type of sword most likely came from China. *Kusanagi no Tsurugi*, the sword of the Imperial Regalia, is this type of sword. These swords fell out of use around 900 CE.

The *warabite-to* was Japan's first curved sword. This style of the sword began to appear around 300 CE. The *warabite-to* was generally less than two feet long. In early versions, the sword had a straight blade with a curved handle. Over time, the sword evolved to become thinner. At the same time, a gentle curve was introduced to the blade.

The *tachi* (or "great sword") along with its smaller counterpart, the *kodachi*, were developed in the 900s CE. The *tachi* was longer than their predecessors at around 30 inches. In this sword, the entire blade is curved. Some scholars hypothesize that the move towards curved blades was to make the blade faster to unsheath and more useful for slashing, especially when wielded from on horseback (*All Types of*

Japanese Swords (history and how they were used), 2020). Another likely reason, however, was due to the introduction of a new process known as "differential hardening." This process made the swords more flexible and less prone to breaking. It also naturally resulted in the curvature of the blade.

During the Muromachi Period, the *uchigatana* (meaning "striking sword") became popular. This sword was less expensive than the *tachi,* making it popular with lower-ranking footsoldiers. These were worn with the blade facing up, allowing the user to draw the sword and strike in one single motion.

Also, during the Muromachi Period, the *katana* (meaning "single blade sword") appeared. This is the sword most

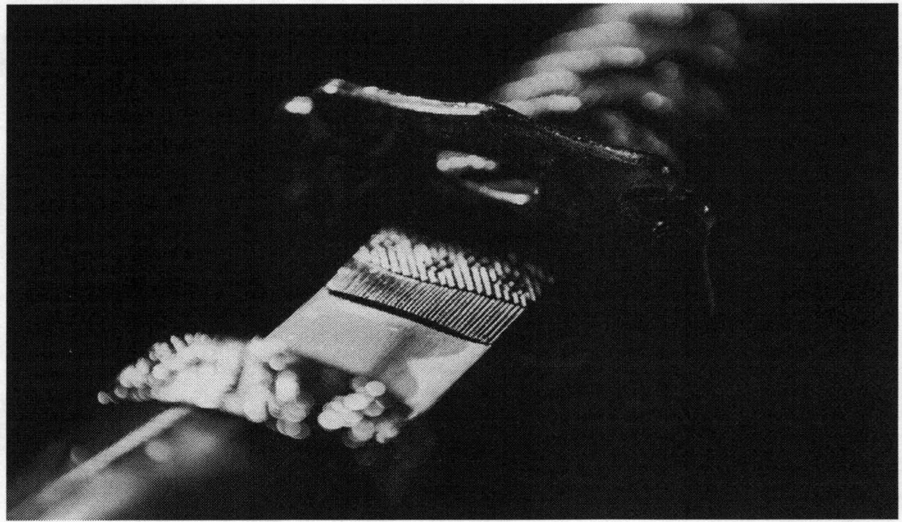

commonly associated with the samurai today. It was around two to three feet long and was less curved than the *uchigatana*. Like the *uchigatana,* the *katana* was worn with the blade facing up, giving it the same benefits of unsheathing and slashing in one motion. While there is a common misconception that the *katana* was a samurai's primary weapon, this is not the case. Weapons, such as the bow and arrow or polearm, were preferred for their greater range. The *katana* was used as a last resort if a samurai was thrown from their horse or if they were fighting indoors.

Another sword of note is the *odachi* (literally "great big sword"), which was a single-bladed sword longer than three feet. It was briefly popular in the late Kamakura Period. This sword was used by samurai on horseback. Due to its length, it had to be worn on the swordsman's back making it difficult to unsheath. Because of its unwieldiness and impracticality, the *odachi* would fall out of use during the Edo Period.

Warring States

Let's return now to our timeline in the Muromachi Period. As we stated at the beginning of this chapter, the new Ashikaga Shogunate had wrested control from Emperor Go-Daigo and the Imperial court. The powerful samurai class was composed of men motivated by personal gain over loyalty to their country. And Japan was on the verge of entering an era of near-constant war. This era was known as the *Sengoku Jidai* or the Warring States period. This was the golden age of the samurai.

In 1464 CE, shogun Ashikaga Yoshimasa had no heir. Therefore, there was no clear successor to replace him at the end of his time as a shogun. To attempt to avoid a potential dispute, he adopted his younger brother Ashikaga Yoshimi. This, he thought, would make for a smooth and peaceful transition of power at the end of his reign. But then, in 1465 CE, Yoshimasa had a son. This surprised Yoshimasa and threw a wrench into his plans of a smooth transition. Yoshimasa's wife, Hino Tomiko, obviously wanted their son to become the next shogun. Yoshimi and his supporters were none too pleased with this development. The debate became heated. This disagreement over who should be the next shogun erupted into armed fighting in 1467 CE in what would become known as the Ōnin War.

The central authority of Japan began to crumble. Daimyo

("regional warlords") scrambled to claim whatever lands they could in the ensuing chaos. Japan lost any semblance of national unity and became an island of roughly 100 warring fiefdoms that would battle for nearly 100 years.

In the Mikawa Province in 1548 CE, the mighty Oda clan invaded the Matsudaira territory. The Matsudaira turned to their nearest neighbor, the Imigawa clan, for help defending their land. The Imigawa agreed to lend their aid, provided their leader, Matsudaira Hirotada, sent his son, Matsudaira Motoyasu, for them to keep as a hostage. Lacking alternatives, Hirotada agreed. However, while Motoyasu was being transported to Imigawa territory, the Oda intercepted him and captured Motoyasu.

The Oda sent a missive to the Matsudaira with the ultimatum to either end their alliance with the Imigawa or they would kill Motoyasu. In a bold move, Hirotada writes back to Oda that they should kill his son if they must. That would only show the Imigawa how strong their alliance truly was. The Oda had not bargained on this. They decided to simply keep Motoyasu alive as a hostage until they could find some use for him.

During a siege by the Imigawa on the Oda clan, they offered to let the head of the Oda clan live if they agreed to hand over the castle they were attacking as well as Motoyasu. The Oda agreed. The Matsudaira leader had just recently passed, making Motoyasu the de facto head of the Matsudaira clan. The Imigawa saw this as a way of further strengthening their alliance with the Matsudaira clan.

When Motoyasu reaches adulthood, the Imigawa return him to the Matsudaira clan. Under his leadership, the Matsudaira along with the Imigawa plowed through the Oda land. Motivated by the success of their campaign, the allied clans set their sights on Kyoto.

Oda Nobunaga

The Oda were nearly defeated. They holed up in a castle prepared for one final stand. Their leader, Oda Nobunaga, gathered roughly 2,500 men to ride out against the roughly 25,000 Imigawa gathered before the castle. Nobunaga sends 500 of his men to create a diversion, pretending all his forces are gathered at a hilltop fort. The remaining 2,000 men launch an ambush on the distracted Imigawa army and slaughter them.

The Matsudaira who had been camping in a separate but nearby area witnessed the slaughter of the mighty Imigawa army at the hands of only a couple thousand Oda warriors. Impressed by this victory against all odds, Motoyasu (who would take the name Tokugawa Ieyasu) went to meet with Nobunaga and the two formed an alliance.

While the other clans to the east were embroiled in conflict amongst themselves, Nobunaga's new alliance with the Matsudaira (later renamed the Tokugawa) provided him a buffer and allowed him to move his troops towards, Kyoto without fear of enemy clans from the east invading Oda territory. Only two clans now stood between Nobunaga and Kyoto: the Azai and the Saito. To secure peace relations with the Azai, Nobunaga married his sister to the Azai's daimyo. Nobunaga also reaches out to his father-in-law, Dosan, who is the daimyo of the Saito clan. But before Dosan was able to formally establish peace between the Saito and Oda clans, he was killed in yet another dispute over succession called the Battle of Nagara-gawa. His successor, Saito Yoshitatsu, rejects any attempt at peace between the Saito and Oda clans.

At this point, it's important to briefly introduce another legendary samurai and daimyo: Toyotomi Hideyoshi. He began life as a lowly peasant before he got his first break as sandal-bearer to Oda Nobunaga. He gained Nobunaga's favor and got promoted to a higher position overseeing castle repairs. Keep an eye out for him, because he played a major role in the events to come.

Inabayama Castle

Back to our timeline, from 1561-1563 CE the Oda and Saito were locked in a fierce battle. The Saito remained deeply entrenched and managed to keep the Oda at bay. Nobunaga enlists the help of Hideyoshi. By this point, Hideyoshi had proven himself to be skilled in diplomacy. He approached Saito leaders and encouraged them one by one to defect to Oda's side. With this massive loss of support, the Saito was severely weakened but still held firm in their mighty fortress of Inabayama Castle. Nobunaga ordered Hideyoshi to construct a fortress for the Oda right at the foot of Inabayama Castle. Hideyoshi was able to construct this fortress too quickly for the Saito to launch an attack against it.

Hideyoshi had learned of a secret path through the mountains that would allow a small number of Oda men to sneak into Inabayama Castle undetected. Undercover of darkness, Hideyoshi and a small group of men successfully snuck into the castle and set fire to the storehouses and armory. The gunpowder in the armory exploded. Then Hideyoshi and his men threw open the gate to the castle, allowing Nobunaga and the rest of the troops to rush in and storm the castle. With the fall of Inabayama Castle, the Saito was defeated. Nobunaga granted Hideyoshi the title of daimyo for his valor and service. The end of the Saito meant the Oda had a clear path to march into Kyoto. The only thing Nobunaga lacked was a moral justification for invading. To invade without a valid reason would risk uniting the other clans against him. He would also risk losing his existing supporters.

Taking Kyoto

The solution to this dilemma came in 1568 CE when Ashikaga Yoshiaki approached Nobunaga. He claimed he was the rightful heir to the office of the shogun. He asked for the support of the Oda to restore him to his proper station. Nobunaga leaped at the opportunity. He publicly declared that he was marching on Kyoto and that anyone standing against him was in defiance of the true shogun of Japan.

The Oda forces had little trouble securing Kyoto and making Yoshiaki shogun. However, Nobunaga had no intention of actually handing over control of Japan to Yoshiaki. Nobunaga made Yoshiaki send invitations to the nearby daimyo to come to a feast in Kyoto. Yoshiaki secretly sent letters to the daimyo stating Nobunaga was a traitor and calling for them to take him out. This, obviously, seemed suspicious to the daimyo. When many of them, such as the Asakura, refused to attend the feast, Nobunaga declared them to be traitors and declared war against them. To reach the Asakura, Nobunaga had to march his troops through Azai territory. Nobunaga assumed this would go smoothly since he had secured their allegiance through marrying his sister to the Azai clan leader. When Nobunaga reached the Azai territory, however, the Azai switched sides to join up with the Asakura clan. Nobunaga was able to split his army and escape, but he vowed vengeance against the treacherous Azai. During their escape, a ninja assassin named Hachisuka Tenzō fired two shots at Nobunaga before slipping off into the woods. The attack was unsuccessful as both bullets lodged in Nobunaga's armor.

In July of 1570 CE, the Oda and Tokugawa forces marched into Azai territory. They approached the Azai's main castles along the Anegawa River, where they were met by the combined Azai and Asakura forces. While the Oda and Tokugawa forces were victorious, the battle left the Oda too weakened to continue their advance, so they retreated to Kyoto. Recognizing how much the Oda forces were weakened, the Miyoshi clan whom the Oda had kicked out of Kyoto saw their chance at revenge. The Miyoshi forged an alliance with a band of militant, Buddhist warrior monks known as the Ikko-Ikki from the temple of Ishiyama Hongan-ji.

Warrior Monks

The Ishiyama Hongan-ji temple, which lay just south of Kyoto, had been a thorn in Nobunaga's side for some time. The monks had refused to pay taxes, disrupted trade, and were a major obstacle in Nobunaga conquering Japan. So Nobunaga, along with 30,000 men, went to surround Ishiyama Hongan-ji temple. When the Oda forces attempted to advance, the muddy marshland slowed their progress. The 3,000 monks armed with arquebuses (an early version of the musket) prevented Nobunaga's troops from advancing further. Unable to take the temple, but also unwilling to admit defeat, Nobunaga's forces camped around the temple for the next 11 years. This became the longest siege in Japan's history.

While all this was going on, the Asakura and Azai allied with another group of warrior monks from Enryaku-ji, a temple on Mount Hiei. Unable to have enemies on all sides, Nobunaga makes a truce with the Asakura and Azai clans. Learning from the 11-year siege at Ishiyama Hongan-ji, Nobunaga decides to demolish the Enryaku-ji temple by setting the forest around it on fire and ordering his troops to kill anyone who tried to flee.

Ieyasu's Most Successful Loss

By 1571 CE, Nobunaga had launched even more campaigns against warrior-monk temples. He was able to use his growing military strength to crush the Azai and Asakura clans. Meanwhile, Shogun Ashikaga Yoshiaki was still pleading for someone to help him take back control from Nobunaga. Answering the call was one of the most famous samurai of the Sengoku Jidai: Takeda Shingen. He planned his own march on Kyoto through Mikawa, Tokugawa Ieyasu's home province. Ieyasu assembled troops to stop Shingen in Mikawa. Ieyasu made the mistake of setting up his arquebusiers on an open plain, leaving them susceptible to Shingen's signature military maneuver: the cavalry charged. The cavalry demolished Ieyasu's forces.

By the time Ieyasu made it back to his castle stronghold, he had only five men remaining. What Ieyasu did next could be considered an act of madness, genius, or perhaps a mixture of the two. He had his men (just five men, remember) light all the lamps along the castle walls. Then, Ieyasu's men opened the castle gates and began to beat drums. Shingen's men were understandably confused. This appeared to them to be some kind of trap. So Shingen's men waited outside the castle. When night fell, Ieyasu sent the now-famous ninja, Hattori Hanzo, and his ninja comrades to attack the Takeda troops and cause confusion. This attack led Shingen and his forces to believe Ieyasu was hiding a great number of men in the castle, so the Takeda retreated.

Nagashino Castle

In 1573 CE, Takeda Shingen once again set his sights on Kyoto and rode with his troops into Mikawa. However, a sniper shot and killed Shingen in battle. Shingen's less adept son, Takeda Katsuyori, took his place. Under Katsuyori, the Takeda attacked Nagashino castle. The Takeda invaders greatly outnumbered the Mikawa defenders and pushed them back into the castle's keep. One of the defenders, a man called Suneemon, volunteered to sneak past the Takeda lines and come back with reinforcements. Suneemon was able to reach Ieyasu and Nobunaga and tell them about the siege. Nobunaga and Ieyasu agreed to come to their aid. Suneemon decided to ride ahead to inform the besieged Mikawa that help was on the way, but the Takeda captured him before he could make it back.

Takeda Katsuyori told Suneemon that he would spare his life if Suneemon agreed to shout to the castle that no help was coming. Suneemon agreed. The following day, the Takeda brought Suneemon out in front of the castle tied to a crucifix. When it came time for him to call out to the castle, he yelled that Nobunaga and Ieyasu were on their way. The Takeda killed Suneemon with spears, but the defenders received his message. Their morale boosted by Suneemon's news, they held the castle. When Ieyasu and Nobunaga's troops arrived, they completely demolished the Takeda forces.

The Takeda forces that did remain, made an alliance with the Uesugi clan and the warrior monks of Ishiyama Hongan-ji. Uesugi Kenshin was considered by his clan to be a living embodiment of the kami of war. However, in 1578 CE, while preparing an invasion of Oda land, Kenshin died of esophageal cancer. With the Uesugi weakened by the loss of their powerful leader, Nobunaga was able to finally defeat the warrior monks of Ishiyama Hongan-ji and what remained of the Takeda clan.

Nobunaga and Ieyasu were touring the Kansai region when they received a request from Hideyoshi for reinforcements for a siege. Nobunaga sent his general Akechi Mitsuhide to lead an army to assist Hideyoshi, while he himself went through Kyoto first to attend to some business there. Nobunaga spent the night in the Honno-ji temple. Mitsuhide marched his army through Kyoto. When they came to Honno-ji temple, Mitsuhide turned traitor. He ordered his men to attack the temple. They massacred Nobunaga's men. Nobunaga retreated to the inner sanctuary, lit it on fire, and committed seppuku rather than being captured.

This left Ieyasu in a precarious situation. He was now in the Kansai region with just a small number of men and the treacherous Mitsuhide army between him and the Tokugawa territory hundred of miles to the east. Fortunately, Ieyasu had the legendary ninja Hattori Hanzo with him. Hanzo was able to show Ieyasu a secret path to sneak around the Mitsuhide forces and finally make his way back to Tokugawa territory.

Mitsuhide, now in control of Kyoto, began to kill anyone he thought posed a threat to his newly stolen power, starting with Nobunaga's family. Hideyoshi got wind of Mitsuhide's betrayal and rode with his army back to Kyoto to crush Mitsuhide's troops. Mitsuhide was killed after officially holding the title of shogun for just three days. The local daimyo met and agreed on an heir to the shogun, the then two-year-old Oda Hidenobu.

This allowed Hideyoshi to become regent and to be the real influence behind the office of the shogun.

Tokugawa Ieyasu agreed to acknowledge Hideyoshi as his lord. In exchange, Hideyoshi granted the Tokugawa special privileges. Importantly, the Tokugawa were exempt from serving in Hideyoshi's army for the next decade.

Hideyoshi held a vision of unified Japan, so he implemented three major reforms. This included revising the tax structure; stripping all peasants of their swords and guns and outlawing them from owning any in the future, and finally establishing a rigid caste system and forbidding anyone from rising up from the caste they were born into. Hideyoshi also instituted a policy that peasants were tied to the land they lived on and could not travel freely. These policies so stabilized Japan that they remained in place more or less unchanged until 1871 CE.

The only remaining issue Hideyoshi faced was what to do about the samurai class. These were, after all, armed warriors whose only profession was killing. So to occupy the samurai, Hideyoshi sent them on a campaign with the insanely ambitious goal of conquering China. The campaign never got further than Korea. Japan had to end the fighting and retreat after losing hundreds of thousands of men with nothing to show for it. The one group of warriors that was spared was the Tokugawa clan. Remember, Hideyoshi had granted them a 10-year exemption from military service.

The End of the Sengoku Jidai

In 1598 CE, Regent Toyotomi Hideyoshi died of an unknown illness. Shortly before his death, he had assembled a group of five feudal lords known as the Council of Five Elders to act as regents for his five-year-old son. Among them was none other than Tokugawa Ieyasu.

Many lords were bitter over the failed Korean campaign and wanted the power to pass to a Tokugawa. Others were afraid of the growing Tokugawa power. Still, some schemed to exploit the fact that a child was a shogun and steal power for themselves.

A former administrator under the late Hideyoshi, a man named Ishida Mitsunari, was one such man who had his eye on the prize of ultimate power. He plotted to assassinate Ieyasu. He also tried to make it seem as though the Maeda clan were co-conspirators in his plot. However, Ieyasu learned of the plot and informed the Maeda. The Maeda pledged their loyalty to Ieyasu and planned to kill Mitsunari. Mitsunari went to Ieyasu to beg for mercy, which Ieyasu granted. However, Mitsunari continued scheming about how he could claim power. He forged an alliance with a mutual enemy of the Tokugawa, the Uesugi.

In 1600 CE, the Uesugi marched into Tokugawa territory under the leadership of Uesugi Kenshin's heir, Uesugi Kagekatsu. Ieyasu's ally, Torii Mototada, held a castle that would almost certainly be one of the first places the enemy attacked as it was between them and Kyoto. Mototada pledged to hold his castle against the invaders knowing full well that he would die in the process. Mototada and his 2,000 men held the castle for 10 days against an invading force of 40,000 strong. Before the castle fell, the Torii had taken a chunk out of the Ishida forces. The 10-day delay allowed Ieyasu to rally his troops and repel the Uesugi.

Then the Ishida and the Tokugawa met at Sekigahara. The forces were evenly matched, neither side had a clear advantage. A division of 16,000 men on the Ishida side under the command of Kobayakawa Hideaki had stayed out of the battle on a hilltop, simply watching. All at once, they rushed down from the mountain and betrayed the Ishida by smashing into their flank, turning the tide of the battle. The Ishida were quickly defeated and the Ieyasu's forces won.

The Emperor granted Ieyasu the title of shogun in 1603 CE. He ruled for just two years before retiring and passing the title of shogun to his son, Tokugawa Hidetada. At this point, Hidetada was an adult who had already proven himself in battle. Because Hidetada was actually a competent leader and his father, the great Ieyasu, was still alive, his authority as shogun went unchallenged.

The only remaining potential threat to Tokugawa power was Toyotomi Hideyori, Hideyoshi's son. Hideyori remained secure in Osaka castle until, in 1614 CE, the Tokugawa decided to attack it and eliminate this one final threat. Osaka castle fell the following year, finally ending the Sengoku Jidai.

CHAPTER 6
EDO AND MEIJI PERIODS

The Edo Period lasted from 1603 to 1867 CE. This time, following the turbulent Sengoku Jidai, was characterized by peace and isolation from the rest of the world. When Tokugawa Ieyasu had finally become shogun, he established the shogunate capital in Edo. He had distributed land amongst the daimyo in a way that would prevent any of them from growing too powerful; he would take land from daimyo who displeased him and give it to daimyo who had earned his favor. He mandated these daimyos spend every other year in Edo, further ensuring their loyalty to the shogunate. The success of these reforms is evident in the 250-year reign of the Tokugawa shogunate and the stability of this era.

Life in Edo Japan

A political system known as bakuhan emerged. Under this system, the shogun held all authority on a national level while the daimyo held authority on the local level. The daimyo was connected to the shogunate through an increasingly complex bureaucracy. The dominant philosophy of the age was

Confucianism, which extolled values such as loyalty and hard work that helped support the rigid caste system Ieyasu had implemented. The social hierarchy went as follows. The emperor was at the top of the social order, though as we've already seen any real power the emperor had was long gone. Below that was the shogun who held all real authority. Beneath the shogun was the daimyo. Under that were the samurai, who were still praised for the valor they had displayed during the Sengoku Jidai but had little chance for heroics in this era of stability and peace. Beneath that were artists, merchants, and peasants.

While the capital still officially remained in Kyoto where the emperor resided, Edo (modern-day Tokyo) was the most important and powerful city in Japan. Given Tokyo's size today, it may be surprising to consider what small and unassuming village Edo was when Tokugawa Ieyasu selected this location for shogunate headquarters in 1603 CE. Since he required all the daimyo to have a second home in Edo. The shogun also stipulated that the daimyo had to leave their wives and children in Edo when they returned to their home provinces. Since Edo became a meeting point for the wealthy elites, artisans and merchants also flooded to the city as they realized the business potential that existed there. The city would grow from just a few thousand residents to become the largest city on Earth by 1721 CE when the population was estimated at around one million. Many public bathhouses (sentō) were built to accommodate the burgeoning population. These became important social centers much as their counterparts in ancient Rome had been.

The dense concentration of wooden houses made Edo prone to the many fires it experienced, notably the Great fire of Meireki in 1657 CE. According to legend, this fire began when a priest attempted to burn a cursed kimono. The three previous owners had all died before they had been able to wear it. When the priest set fire to the kimono, a gust of wind spread the flames. Before anything could be done to stop it, nearby buildings caught fire. This ensuing conflagration destroyed roughly two-thirds of the city and claimed 100,000 lives. In the aftermath, the government instituted new safety standards and reorganized the city to prevent any recurrence of such a tragedy.

Like in the prior Heian Period, this era of peace allowed people to appreciate the natural beauty of Japan. Cherry blossoming viewing (hanami) and moon viewing (otsukimi) became popular pastimes for people of all social classes. The merchant class did especially well during this time. They were flush with cash from the growing wealth of Edo. At the same time, they weren't held to the same moral standards as the samurai or daimyo classes. They enjoyed lavish, hedonistic lifestyles in the city's growing pleasure districts. There was a proliferation of erotic artwork set in these brothel districts known as ukiyo-e, literally "floating world art." The "floating world" referred to the lifestyle of seeking transient worldly pleasures. During the Edo Period, the technique of woodblock printing (mokuhanga) allowed for works of art to be mass-produced, driving down the price and making art more accessible than ever before. One very famous example from the late Edo Period is the iconic woodblock print called The Great Wave off Kanagawa, a work by Hokusai as part of his ambitious project Thirty-six Views of Mount Fuji. Kabuki theater also began during the Edo Period and was popular entertainment for the lower and merchant classes.

The Tokugawa shogunate initially supported trade with foreign nations but was wary of foreigners and foreign ideas. Ieyasu had sought to make the ports of Edo the main port for foreign traders, but Europeans opted to use ports in Kyushu instead. This posed a threat to the authority of the Edo government. At the same time, Daimyo in and around Kyushu began to convert to Christianity, a foreign ideology that posed a threat to the caste system. After finally achieving stability and control, the Tokugawa shogunate was not about to let foreigners destabilize the country once again. By 1616 CE, Christianity was forbidden. And finally, the Closed Country Edict of 1635 CE was implemented. This strict order forbade Japanese people from leaving the country and any who had left from returning. In 1637 CE, overtaxed peasants and unhappy Christians took up arms in what would be known as the Shimabara Rebellion. A large number of unhappy samurai came to aid the rebels and fought so tenaciously that the 100,000 Japanese men sent by the shogun were unable to quash the rebellion. Finally, the shogun was able to enlist the help of the Dutch East India Company who supplied the weapons. They were finally able to quash the rebellion. For their help, The Netherlands got the exclusive right to be the only western country Japan traded with for the next two and a half centuries. Likely experiencing flashbacks from the Sengoku Jidai, the Tokugawa shogunate aggressively closed its borders to the dangerous and destabilizing foreigners.

This ushered in a period of extreme isolation known as sakoku ("locked country") that lasted for over 250 years. The policy of Japanese isolationism would last until it was brought to an end in 1853 CE by U.S. Commodore Matthew C. Perry.

Commodore Perry Opens Japan

If anyone was qualified for the difficult task of opening Japan to foreign trade, it was Commodore Matthew C. Perry. Born in Rhode Island, USA in 1794 CE, Perry had a decorated naval career. He had served aboard the USS Cyane in 1820 CE, carrying freed Black slaves to help establish the country of Liberia. He patrolled African waters to suppress pirates and slave traders. He was an avid proponent of naval education and the then-novel technology of steam-powered ships, earning him the moniker "The Father of the Steam Navy." He had negotiations with the top admiral of the Turkish Navy, the kingdom of Naples, the President of Liberia, African chiefs, Mexican tribal leaders, and the British Navy. Tsar Nicholas I of Russia was so impressed with Perry, he offered him a position as an admiral in the Russian Navy.

Prior to 1852 CE, Japanese policy against foreign ships landing in Japan was so extreme that even shipwreck survivors who washed ashore would be imprisoned or even executed. This provided America some justification for forcing a trade agreement with Japan. It's also worth noting that America was in the era of Manifest Destiny, where they were growing and expanding with virtually no end in sight. They had also profited tremendously from the opium trade with China. This had led to the Opium Wars, which showcased the military might of western powers and would have rightly given Japan cause for alarm.

In 1852 CE, US President Millard Fillmore assigned Perry the task of persuading Japan to agree to safely return shipwrecked American sailors, allowing U.S. ships to dock in Japan to take on coal and water, and most importantly opening Japan to foreign trade. President Fillmore gave Perry complete authority to secure the best terms with Japan he could.

In 1853 CE, he arrived with the first steam-powered ships the Japanese had ever seen. The Japanese referred to these as kurofune ("black ships"). The Japanese Navy surrounded these boats and ordered Perry and his men to leave. Perry refused to leave until he was allowed to deliver a letter from President

Fillmore to Emperor Kōmei. Claiming he was celebrating the U.S. Independence Day, Perry had all his ships fire off blanks and explosive cannonballs. The Japanese, feeling now that negotiation was necessary to their survival, ultimately allowed Perry to land in Kurihama on July 14, 1853. Having delivered the letter, Perry promised he would return for a reply the following year.

Perry returned in 1854 CE with an even larger naval force. When he landed on March 8th, Perry made a point to make the greatest show of it he could. He sent three bands to march ahead of him in formation playing the Star-Spangled Banner. Perry himself marched outflanked by two of the largest African-American sailors in his squadron, a completely novel sight in sakoku era Japan. When negotiations began, the Japanese delegates agreed to allow U.S. ships to land at two specific ports to take on coal and water. They also agreed to return the imprisoned U.S. sailors. But they did not yet agree to open trade relations with America.

At this point, the U.S. and Japanese exchanged gifts with one another. Perry had come prepared with some gifts intended to tantalize Japan into considering what wonders they could expect if they opened trade with the U.S. Perry gave gifts of modern revolvers, rifles, two telegraph sets, and Perry's pièce de résistance, a fully functional ¼ scale railroad and engine. To celebrate the signing of the treaty, both sides gave great feasts with large quantities of food and alcohol. One story goes that one of the intoxicated Japanese commissioners came up to Perry and threw his arm around Perry's neck and ruined Perry's epaulets. He told Perry through an interpreter "Japan and America. All the same heart." One of Perry's men asked why Perry had tolerated this. Perry reportedly replied, "Oh, if they will only sign the treaty, he may kiss me" (Morison, 1967).

On March 31, 1854, both the U.S. and Japan signed the Treaty of Kanagawa. But the U.S. wasn't satisfied that they hadn't secured trading rights with Japan, so in 1858 CE another U.S. envoy named Townsend Harris negotiated just such an agreement with the Harris Treaty. This effectively ended Japan's period of isolation. This ushered in an era when an unindustrialized Japan was strong-armed into a series of unequal treaties with the industrialized West.

Meiji Restoration

While the Edo Period had been an era of peace, it had also been a pressure cooker with tensions boiling just beneath the surface. All the strict policies the Tokugawa shogunate implemented served to maintain the status quo within Japan for centuries. They had also managed to deal with foreign policy by sticking their fingers in their ears and ignoring how the rest of the world had been modernizing. But now the West had shown up at their doorsteps with warships and weapons and buffaloed their way in. Within Japan, there was growing unrest as well.

Virtually all of the wealth and cultural benefits we described in the previous section were limited to Edo. In the provinces, peasants were forced to remain on their land incurring heavy taxes and famine while the samurai class enjoyed leisure time and wrote poetry. The samurai looked on as the merchant class that was supposedly beneath them in status lived lavish lifestyles and partied in brothels.

As we stated previously, the Dutch were the one western nation that Japan traded with during the period of isolation. Rangaku ("Dutch studies") served as the sole link between Japan and Western knowledge during this time. Intellectuals became fascinated with these new and innovative ideas, especially in the fields of science and technology. This would help form the foundation for the rapid technological advancement to come.

Now the daimyo watched as the supposedly powerful shogun kowtowed to western power and signed unequal treaties left and right. Their loyalty began to wane. Realizing the need to modernize if they wanted to survive, Shogun Tokugawa Iemochi opened schools to study Western thought and technology. At the same time, what could be described as a nationalist, an anti-Western terrorist group called the shishi ("men of great purpose") began to form in the southern province of Choshu with the rallying cry sonnō jōi ("revere the emperor, expel the barbarians"). They began to assassinate westerners and fire on western ships attempting to land in Japanese harbors. In 1864 CE, the shishi even tried to take Kyoto. They were unsuccessful, but the writing was on the wall. The absolute control the Tokugawa shogunate had wielded was rapidly beginning to crumble. The shishi soon realized that Western influence was here to stay whether they liked it or not. So they adopted the new motto: wakon yōsai ("Japanese spirit, western technology").

Meanwhile, U.K. Diplomat Sir Harry Parkes consulted with Japanese samurai and diplomat Saigō Takamori to discuss how British weapons and tactics could be used to rebel against the shogunate. In 1866 CE, Tokugawa Iemochi died and was succeeded by a new shogun, Tokugawa Yoshinobu. The following year, Emperor Kōmei died of an unknown illness and was succeeded by then 14-year-old Emperor Meiji.

With this swift political restructuring, the pro-imperial (anti-shogunate) clans of the Satsuma and the Chōshū formed an alliance known as the Satchō Alliance with the stated purpose of killing Shogun Yoshinobu and restoring the power of the emperor. When Yoshinobu discovered this, he offered to step down to take a position beneath the emperor as the head of the council. The Satchō Alliance refused and called for him to completely renounce all political power. So in 1868 CE, Yoshinobu stepped down declaring a full restoration of all imperial power.

However, Yoshinobu wasn't content to give up without a fight. He rallied the daimyo who were still loyal to him and went to war in an event known as the Boshin War. On January 27, 1868, the shogunate forces attacked Kyoto. While the Imperial forces were outnumbered, they had the benefit of modern weapons (such as rifles, Gatling guns, and howitzers), and were able to repel the attackers. Some of the daimyo loyal to the shogun began to defect after seeing the power of these modern weapons. By May of that year, the Satchō Alliance had reclaimed Edo and forced the former shogun to surrender. Yoshinobu was stripped of his land and titles and put under house arrest. Even so, a coalition of clans to the north refused to surrender to imperial rule. Once again, the imperial arsenal of modern weapons allowed them to crush the last of the anti-imperialist resistance by October of that year. The imperial court was moved to the thriving metropolis of Edo, which was renamed

Tokyo ("eastern capital"). The last vestiges of the resistance retreated to Hokkaido and were defeated five months later. This "restoring" of power to the emperor is the reason this era is often called the Meiji Restoration, though, in truth, it was the first time all of Japan truly had a single centralized government.

Now that this power dispute was settled, Japan had an even bigger task on its hands. The protracted period of isolation had left the country centuries behind the industrialized West. In order to be relevant on the world stage, Japan had to do in decades what had taken the West centuries. They quickly implemented public education, discarded the caste system in favor of social mobility, and replaced the samurai with a conscription army which all able-bodied men had to serve for 3 years. The new focus for Japan would be national pride instead of a feudal hierarchy.

The samurai were not pleased to be stripped of their rank. Saigō Takamori's home province of Satsuma became a hotbed of discontent. When a plot by the Imperial government to assassinate Takamori was discovered, an armed group left for Kyoto to demand an explanation. The following battles would be known as the Satsuma Rebellion. In 1877 CE, while on the way to Kyoto, they encountered Kumamoto Castle and their advance was halted. They laid siege to the castle but were eventually repelled by the new conscript army. The samurai were driven back to Kagoshima, where they made their final stand at the Battle of Shiroyama. The new conscript army outnumbered the samurai 60-to-1. Takamori and his men fought until the last man fell dead, ending in a final suicide charge of just 40 samurai against the mighty conscription army.

Takamori would be remembered as a tragic hero and the last great samurai warrior. Putting down this rebellion was so costly to the Imperial government that they were forced to abandon the gold standard.

Meanwhile, Japan was rapidly industrializing. Massive public works projects were underway putting in railways and telephone infrastructure. The emperor hired consultants from across Europe to guide Japan in this period of rapid modernization. Women were still held as inferior to men and expected to hold their "traditional" roles as wives, mothers, and housekeepers. But everyone, including women, was given four years of public education. This enabled the nation to standardize the Japanese language across the country and help promote national identity through a common curriculum. Public schools were also able to incorporate an expanded version of the Bushido code to promote the virtues of honor and service.

The western influence could also be seen in art. New western-inspired art that focused on realism was called yōga ("western-style paintings") as distinct from nihonga ("Japanese-style paintings"). Western styles of architecture were incorporated into Japan's growing cities as well. In 1889 CE, the ban on playing cards was lifted which allowed a company called Nintendo (yes, that Nintendo) to begin producing them. In the midst of all this rapid change, there was a very real fear that Japan was losing its national identity. The one defining trait of the Japanese national identity that the people could rally around was the emperor. In 1889 CE, Japan adopted its first constitution. They set up a cabinet, prime minister, and bicameral legislature. But even these were seen as gifts from the emperor.

Even as Japan was incorporating advancements and

technology from the west, they sought to assert their uniquely Japanese sense of identity. Japan used this as justification for expanding their empire by "liberating" other Asian countries from western control by conquering them. To this end, Japan annexed the Ryukyu Islands in 1879 CE. In 1894 CE, Japan overtook Korea. When China attempted to help liberate Korea from Japanese control, the newly modernized Japan easily repelled the Chinese forces. Japan then annexed Taiwan. In 1904 CE, Russia challenged Japan for control of Manchuria and Korea. Japan offered a compromise, but Russia refused. In the ensuing Russo-Japanese War, Japan demolished Russia in the first-ever victory of an Asian nation over a western power in modern times.

CHAPTER 7
TAISHO PERIOD THROUGH WWII

Emperor Meiji died in 1912 CE after 44 years as emperor. The throne was peacefully passed to Emperor Taishō, who was largely kept out of the public eye due to neurological ailments likely brought about by a childhood case of cerebral meningitis. Even so, the Japanese Empire continued to grow. At the end of the First World War, Japan was represented at the Treaty of Versailles though they were largely ignored. Britain and France claimed massive amounts of land for themselves, while the Japanese presented a racial equality clause to be included in the preamble to the new League of Nations. They hoped to secure for themselves an equal seat at the negotiation table. This clause was roundly rejected by the Council. This slight poured gasoline on the fire of Japan's anti-Western sentiment.

Invading China

In 1932 CE, Japan invaded Manchuria before pushing forward into China. On September 27, 1940, Japan signed the Tripartite Pact with Italy and Germany and officially joined Germany and Italy to form the Axis Powers of World War II. The reasons Japan joined were varied. Most of the Allied Powers, especially the U.S., disapproved of Japan's conquest of China. Japan was still reeling from the exclusion of its equality clause from the League of Nations. It seemed obvious to Japan that the Allied Powers would never treat them as equals. Japan also felt war with the Western powers was inevitable and felt an alliance with Italy and Germany would help deter the U.S. from coming to China's aid. The other major threat to Japan's conquest of China was Russia.

Japan wanted Russia to join the Axis powers, but Germany refused, so instead Japan and Russia signed a nonaggression pact. Another reason Japan joined the Axis Powers was that Germany had just annexed the Netherlands and France. Japan feared that this would mean Germany would soon control the French Indo-China and the Dutch East Indies. Japan desperately needed resources from these regions. It is also worth noting that, at the time Japan signed the Tripartite Pact, it was perfectly reasonable to assume that Germany was going to win the war.

Japan used this opportunity to declare a region of control for themselves known as the Greater East Asia Co-Prosperity Sphere (GEACPS).

In 1940 CE, the U.S. placed an oil embargo on Japan to try and arrest their growing power. Japan retaliated by bombing several U.S. naval sites, most famously Pearl Harbor. This event prompted the U.S. to formally enter World War II.

War Crimes

The Second World War was an extremely dark time for Japan. During this war, Japan committed unspeakable atrocities for which the Japanese government has still never taken full responsibility. In the final days of the war, Japan began burning documents concerning "comfort women."

Between 1932 and 1945 CE, between 100,000 to 200,000 women and girls were trafficked into sex slavery. These women were sent to government-sanctioned "comfort stations," where they were beaten and raped, sometimes as often as 40 times per day by members of the Japanese military. When it became clear that the existing supply of sex workers in Japan would not be enough to satisfy the Japanese army, they began posting fake job advertisements for positions such as secretaries and nurses with the promise of high salaries. Women who applied for these jobs would instead be forced to become sex slaves. When this ruse was discovered, the government began paying gangs to supply them with women. The gangs would procure these women often by simply snatching them off the street (Why Japan Got off Easy in WW2 - The HORRIBLE Atrocities of the Japanese Empire, 2021).

Another black mark on Japanese history from this era comes from the doctors who worked for the Epidemic Prevention and Water Purification Department of the Kwantung Army, more commonly known as Unit 731. This group based in Northern China conducted depraved and nightmarish experiments on civilians and POWs. All of these experiments were officially sanctioned by Emperor Hirohito (later known as Emperor Showa). The stated purpose of these experiments was to learn how the human body responded to various diseases under various conditions. Almost all of the people used in their experiments were healthy individuals. Many were infected with diseases and then dissected while still alive. They forcibly impregnated women, so that they could see the effects of their experiments on mothers and their fetuses. The experimenter replaced living human blood with animal blood or seawater, burned or electrocuted them, used a centrifuge to spin them to death, along with a myriad of other bizarre and grotesque experiments.

One practical purpose of Unit 731 was to identify what pathogens could be used in biological warfare against the Allied Forces, specifically the United States. General Ishii was weeks away from implementing a plan to airdrop fleas infected with this pathogen over the U.S. when Japan surrendered.

At the end of the war, U.S. General MacArthur granted all those involved with Unit 731 a full pardon in exchange for their research. The research was later deemed to be too unscientific to be of any medical use.

Nanjing Massacre

The Japanese also committed what was known as the Nanjing Massacre or the Rape of Nanking, a six-week period of slaughter and rape by the Japanese army beginning December 13, 1937. In the course of this event, the Japanese killed anywhere from 30,000 to 400,000 Chinese. This incident is one of the worst cases of mass rape in recorded history. Many of those targeted by the Japanese soldiers were high school students. Contests were held to see who could cut off the most heads in a given amount of time. In some cases, women were literally raped to death.

Even today, the national war memorial to Japanese servicemen who died from 1868 to 1954 at Yasukuni Shrine displays the names of over 1,000 known war criminals out of the over 2 million names displayed. There is no acknowledgment of their crimes. Some 14 of these are class-A war criminals. Japan's crimes in WWII are still heavily propagandized to this day. Though most modern Japanese do acknowledge the atrocities, some far-right nationalist groups still deny them.

On august 6, 1945, the united states dropped the first atomic bomb on hiroshima. The bomb killed between 70,000-80,000 people, around 50,000-60,000 of whom were civilians. Over 90% of doctors and nurses in hiroshima were killed in the bombing. After the bombing, u.s. president harry s. Truman announced, "if they do not now accept our terms, they may expect a rain of ruin from the air, the like of which has never been seen on this earth" (truman statement on hiroshima, n.d.). Baron kantarō suzuki reiterated japan's commitment to never surrender. Three days later, on august 9, 1945, the u.s. dropped a second atomic bomb on nagasaki. The death toll estimates for the second bombing range between 39,000 to 80,000. On august 14, 1945, emperor hirohito officially surrendered.

U.S.A

CHAPTER 8
POSTWAR PERIOD

At the end of the war, the most pressing issue facing the Japanese people was starvation. The dissolution of the Japanese Empire meant Japan no longer had access to the foreign food supplies they had come to depend on. U.S. General MacArthur was tasked with disarming and democratizing Japan. MacArthur found it advantageous to keep Emperor Hirohito in place to keep the support of the Japanese people. At the Tokyo War Crime Trials of 1946, Prime Minister Hideki Tojo and other military leadership received most of the blame. Japan's military was disarmed and Shinto was removed as the state religion. Previously imprisoned political dissenters were freed and women were given the right to vote. Over a third of the farmland in Japan was purchased from large landlords and corporate entities that held it and were resold to farmers at low prices. This allowed millions of farmers to become landowners and the old feudal system of land ownership crumbled.

The U.S. Army also spearheaded the creation of a new

constitution that guaranteed general elections, free speech, freedom of religion, the right to a fair trial, and womens' suffrage. The first free elections in Japan were held on April 10,

1946. Shigeru Yoshida became the first democratically elected prime minister of Japan. His policies focused on rebuilding Japan's lost infrastructure and on economic growth. At this time, Japan relied completely on the U.S. military for protection against foreign threats. The money not spent on the military was used towards industrial expansion. Japan's economy received another massive boost as Japan supplied materials for the war.

Economic Miracle and Burst Bubble

As a result of the improved infrastructure and new technology, the Japanese economy was transformed into a consumer economy. The government invested large sums into social welfare and education. As a result, the workforce became highly productive. Factories began to produce automobiles, steel, electronics, and tech. Japan gained a reputation for reliability and precision in its manufacturing. By the 1960s, Japanese goods were in high demand and the country found itself in a trade surplus, exporting more products than it was importing. The soaring economy that resulted was known as the Economic Miracle. In just two short decades, Japan had gone from a war-torn, occupied country in shambles to one of the most developed and prosperous countries in history. The U.S. even feared Japan would eclipse America's economy.

In the 1970s, Japan's economic growth slowed. An event known as the OPEC Oil Embargo hit hard, as Japan depended heavily on foreign oil. Even so, the economy still grew throughout the decade. By the 1980s, the country's per capita GDP was greater than that of the U.S. This growth begat speculation that led to a massive housing bubble.

By the 90s, the bubble finally burst. A recession ensued and the economy stagnated. With decreased purchasing power, consumers bought fewer goods which meant the price of goods had to increase since fewer were being sold. This further compounded the problem. The deflation that began in this period still affects Japan to this day.

Today, Japan has one of the oldest populations in the world. The country currently has a population of roughly 147 million, but due partially to a low birth rate this number is projected to fall below 100 million by 2049. This loss of population could mean an economic downturn is on the horizon for Japan, but if history shows us anything, it is the resilience of this nation. Through new technology and expanding opportunities for foreign workers wanting to enter the country, Japan will very likely find a way.

CONCLUSION

Now finally, we have reached the end of our history of Japan. Let's take a moment to recap what we've learned.

We've examined Japan as it grew from its early origins as a hunter-gatherer society with the Jomon People. We've seen the Yayoi bring technology, such as metalworking from China, and start an elaborate network of permanent settlements. We learned the legends behind the Imperial Regalia, or Three Treasures, that represent the divinity of Japan's emperor. We discovered the Nara period when the Fujiwara clan began their rise to power and Japanese writing became widespread. We saw how the peace of the Heian Period allowed for innovations in art such as the first-ever novel.

We studied the Genpei War, where Japan's first shogunate rose to power. We saw Japan repel not one, but two Mongol invasions. We learned about the samurai and saw them battle for 150 years during Japan's turbulent Warring States period. We learned of life under the peaceful, but a strict rule of the Tokugawa shogunate in the Edo Period. We saw Japan isolate itself from the rest of the world for roughly 250 years. Then, we watched as the country reopened trade and modernized at an unprecedented rate.

We saw the emperor return to power during the Meiji Restoration, followed by an overflow of nationalism. We saw Japan join the Axis Powers and go down a dark chapter in her history. Then we saw how this led to the nation's postwar rebuild and created one of the largest economies in the modern-day.

This has been a complex journey, but we hope we have summarized it in a complete and interesting way. Whether you are a scholar or a history enthusiast, hopefully, you have been able to see the history of Japan in a new light. If there's one thing to take away from this book, it's that Japan's history is a story that deserves to be remembered.

THE HISTORY OF INDIA

INTRODUCTION

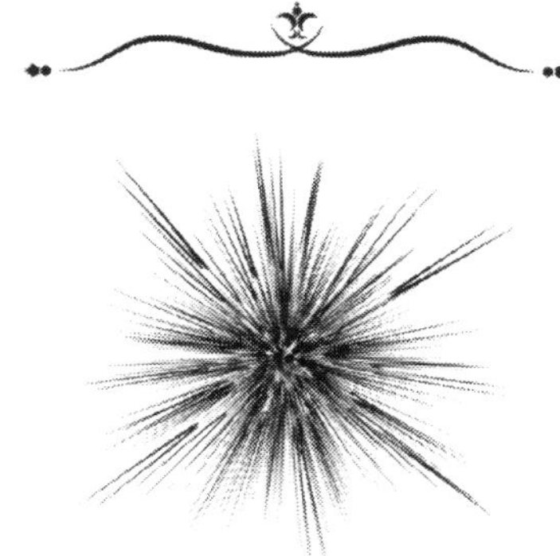

India is a land of stories—of grandeur, bravery, pride, and heritage. It is for this reason that it has been referred to as *Bharata-Varsha,* or the Bharata's land, a beloved king from the Puranic traditions. Those are the cultural roots that this peninsular region grows from.

And yet, Indian history has puzzled scores of historians over the last several years. One of the oldest civilizations on the earth has also proven to be one of the most mysterious. For a long time, this civilization that is the source of a tremendously rich heritage has had quite a fragmented record of its evolution. An interested reader for a long time would find patches of great buzz followed by a lull. And this has been a challenge that historians have been trying to overcome.

When looking at history though, it isn't enough to uncover written records. We also need to pay attention to the mindset of the people who produced those records, the lives they lived, the problems they encountered, their spiritual, philosophical influences, and so on. The point of history is not only uncovering facts but uncovering a life lived by people. And whatever gaps the resources may have on Indian historical facts, we have come to hold an increasingly better understanding of the life that people led in this part of the world.

The amount of progress we have made in the last five decades or so is remarkable. That is not to say we have unearthed some astonishing new evidence that wasn't there before. What we have done though is brought together all kinds of records that were uncovered as well as engaged in interdisciplinary exchange to create an all-around understanding. We have borrowed information from architecture and archeology along with studying inscriptions, written text, and coins. But no matter the sources, historians who bring these sources to life in the form of stories deserve all the praise there is.

As we base this book on these same stories, we hope to pay my tribute to all those who have worked tirelessly to tell us more about this brilliant place. Along with that, with this book, we also wish to produce a more concise, cohesive, and smoother recreation of the growth of the Indian subcontinent through the various ages.

Religious Texts as Historical Sources

One thing people living in any historical age seem to have cared about deeply is religion. And you see this care in the amount of effort they put in compiling their religious texts. Evaluating the validity of these texts might be a difficult proposition. But they do provide us with the tools to understand people's psychological mindset when writing the text. This in turn tells us a lot about their lifestyle. For instance, evaluating the Indian Vedas tells us a lot about the spiritual beliefs of the Hindus at that time and also their rituals.

Samhitas, or the four Vedas—Rig Veda, Sama Veda, Yajur Veda, and Atharva Veda—along with the Brahmanas provide us with valuable insights into the philosophical and spiritual world of the Hindus. Other than that, Upanishads examine the existential nature of the Universe, Smritis are narrated from memory (like Manusmriti, Vishnu Smriti, etc.), the Puranas tell the stories of bravery of different famous kings, and many others provide us with more insight. It needs to be remembered, though, that these are ultimately human creations and may not be what happened but what was perceived or remembered or even imagined, in the case of epics like Mahabharata and Ramayana.

Sometimes, cross-matching with other sources helps build a picture. For example, we also have the Buddhist and the Jain scriptures which may provide just as much valuable information when compared as they would individually, maybe even more.

Despite their proneness to inaccuracy, these certainly cannot be discarded and have provided historians with amazing insights into past civilizations.

An Overview of This Book

This book attempts to look at the history of India in an unfragmented manner, right from the beginning until modern times. Note that the book does not dwell for too long in any of the topics, especially because this is designed to be a beginning reference. Often when people try to absorb too much at once, things stop making sense, especially with history where so many things might be happening at the same time and may be equally important to understand the big picture. The purpose of this book is to help you see the entire picture with as much ease as possible. If you wish to learn more, it might be helpful to keep this book as a reference for understanding the chronology of events coming together and then refer to some more advanced volumes on the desired topic.

Let's begin the journey!

PART 1
ANCIENT INDIA

In this part, we decipher the early Indus civilizations of Harappa and Mohenjo-Daro and their contribution to early Indian history. We also shed light on the bridging period between the ancient and the medieval world, which was dominated by two great dynasties—the Mauryas and the Guptas.

CHAPTER 1

EMERGENCE OF CIVILIZATIONS

There is a story in the Hindu tradition that talks about Manu (regarded as the first man in the Puranas). It talks of the time when Manu is drinking water from a pond and he encounters a fish in his palms when he scoops up water. The fish tells him how scared it is that it will be devoured by the bigger fish and urges him to raise it separately until it becomes bigger. In return, it forewarns Manu of the coming deluge. Manu then built a boat which he entered when the flood drowned everything and the fish steered the boat atop a mountain. So, Manu was saved from the disaster, and with his wife, who appeared out of the ocean water, went on to propagate the human race.

The resemblance of this Puranic myth to Noah's ark may not be a coincidence. Many cultures across the globe have documented a similar catastrophe in their mythology. In the present context, this is important because many historians believe this event to have occurred in 3102 BC after which Manu headed the human race as their first great king.

But keeping the gray blend of history and mythology aside,

if we focus solely on facts, we uncover a different story that may be patchy and rough around the edges but can at least be corroborated by solid evidence.

The Evolution Through the Ages

Multiple excavation sites across India leave no doubt that this subcontinent had its own Paleolithic men. Crude tools made of "Quartzite," a specific type of rock, have been discovered in many parts. These men and women are likely to have led the same stone-age life as their counterparts on the other side of the world. They were nomadic tribes moving from one cave to another in constant fear of dangerous wild animals and hunting and gathering food as they went. Sources estimate these were stout, dark, curly-haired people to be of the Negrito race and that they were far removed from any understanding of "civilization."

However, as evolution progressed and the future generations of these men and women stepped into the Neolithic age, things changed to an unrecognizable degree. The Indian Neolithic society seems to have made tremendous progress over their rock-wielding ancestors. These Neolithic people had a great talent for agriculture and animal domestication. The days of a vagrant lifestyle were thus over and the age of settlements had begun. Though they had not yet mastered housing, they showed great signs of human evolution. They still lived in cave-like structures but now their caves were decorated with stories in the form of paintings and engravings. They made pottery, clothes, carpentry, and even buried their dead in tombs known as "dolmens." The aim was no more just survival but community and communication. The Neolithic settlements at Burzahom in Srinagar in Jammu and Kashmir are the largest of the many settlements found across the subcontinent.

Despite the discovery of many sites, the information we have on these is still quite limited and is thus characterized as prehistoric, i.e. lacking in a documented record of events. But these archeological findings are enough to let us know that even before the so-called civilizations came about, these people were quite sophisticated in their lifestyle.

Ushering In a New Age

The transition through the ages was, of course, not a smooth one. But today, there is little to no doubt that these Neolithic people were the ancestors of those that brought in the new-age civilizations. While even these new-age civilizations were massively different from our modern societies, they still had some peculiar aspects which made all the future progress possible. The use of metals turned out to be one of these aspects. The use of copper and iron came to be a significant factor in the ushering of the Indus Valley Civilization.

For a long time, almost until the 1920s, the existence of this civilization was completely unknown to us. What's more is when the mounds of Mohenjo-Daro in Sind were discovered, the discoverers didn't even believe they were from the ancient era. That really suggests that these settlements didn't have fancy architectural structures but rather a city that bustled with trade and culture. The houses may not have been examples of aesthetically engaging architecture, but the planning of these settlements was immaculate, to say the least.

These cities flourished on the banks of the Indus river and thus came to be known as the Indus Valley civilization. The fertile soil made agriculture quite a lucrative activity. Trade flourished and the wealth in these cities grew. But unfortunately, the civilization was not immune to natural calamities and war. Some sources say that a massive flood in 2000 BC ruined the settlements beyond repair and the civilization began to decline, finally disappearing around 1700 BC. On the other hand, some other sources approximate that this civilization was razed to the ground in a war somewhere in the 15th and 14th centuries BCE. And still, others believed the civilization was around as late as 1300 BC. Whatever the cause, this civilization remains one of the boldest highlights in the history of ancient India.

The People

Though the settlements began flourishing at the banks of the river, they eventually covered a lot of ground in present-day India and Pakistan. Harappa and Mohenjo-Daro, now located in Pakistan, and Dholavira and Banawali, located in India, were the biggest of the cities of this remarkable civilization.

It's interesting to note that the race of the people in the Indus civilization remains largely unknown. Multiple theories link these people to Elamo Dravidians, the early Munda tribe, and even to the Vedic Aryans, but each of these theories leaves significant gaps in the big picture. Thus, the current understanding is that people of all races inhabited this civilization, though their genetic roots are yet uncertain.

The Lifestyle

The people in this civilization seem to have lived quite a modern and luxurious life. They seem to have had a busy economic, social, religious, and even political life. Though we have no written record for any of this from this time period, the articles unearthed from these sites provide us with detailed insight into the lifestyle of the people.

People consumed a plant and animal-based diet, with locally grown wheat, meat like hens, lamb, pork, and freshly-caught fish. Cotton was commonly used for clothing. They used jewelry items like bracelets and necklaces which have been excavated. Small wheeled carts were used as children's toys, and copper and bronze vessels and articles were used for cooking. They even domesticated animals like sheep, elephants, camels, and buffaloes.

It seems they were advanced not only in social life but also in weaponry—they had elaborate weaponry made out of metal. Though there were axes, spears, and bows and arrows, there were interestingly no swords in use. Seals were used for trade not only with locations in India but even globally.

The most intriguing part of their lifestyle was the interest they took and the time they invested in artistic activities. Their beautiful pottery made with a pottery wheel was a considerable advancement from the crude stone implements. Since the pottery items were used commonly in households, this form of artistry was quite integrated with the Harappan lifestyle. Not only that, but there were also masons, carpenters, and goldsmiths who found ways to incorporate art into the articles of daily use.

There is one aspect though that stands out. Despite the advancement, as mentioned before, there were no architecturally monolithic structures in this civilization. Many historians have pondered over why this could be. The answer lies in the geographical nature of these sites. As they were situated on the banks of a river, they had quite the scarcity of stone. The material used for building their houses was kiln-burnt bricks. Though making such bricks was technologically remarkable for those times, it still did not provide the structure with the strength that stones do. Thus, rather than building taller structures, the Harappans preferred to spread out their construction.

The planning of these cities has a particularly modern, urban feel to them. The roads were built in the form of grids with the narrower lanes joining the broad main roads at right angles. There were granaries, great baths, and a brilliant sewage system that was connected even to the smaller houses.

When it came to the religious affiliations of the Harappans, evidence has been found to point to the practice of animism or worship of inanimate natural elements like stone, water, wind, rain, etc. In other words, the Harappans did not seem to have many gods that resembled the Hindu gods that were worshipped in later times. However, there was one god and one goddess, the remains of which have been repeatedly found across the sites, which seemed to be quite similar to the Hindu god Shiva and Hindu Goddess Shakti. Nevertheless, historians today agree that the religious practices of the people of this civilization laid the foundation for Hinduism which was to come into existence in the coming centuries.

The Vedic Transition

While the Indus Valley civilization blossomed in its urban and contemporary lifestyle, there was yet another civilization getting stronger up north from the Harappan culture. One would think it would have shared at least some similarities with its neighbors but the remains unearthed from the ruins of these settlements tell quite a different story. These people called themselves the Aryas of the Aryans. These settlements did not have any of the urban, modern features of the Harappan cities.

It was the Aryan civilization that is considered the basis of Hinduism as it came to be known later. The animism decreases and names of deities like Vishnu, Indra, etc. start showing up. This community had a patriarchal nature which was again contradictory to the equal status given to all in the Harappan culture. Moreover, their literary texts known as Vedas proved to be a significant source for understanding Hinduism. Unfortunately, as with a lot of ancient Indian literary sources, historians have had disagreements about when the first of these, Rig Veda, was written, making the chronological sequence of events a tad foggy.

The collectivistic values of the modern Indian culture are the product of the family life practiced in the Aryan settlements. While women were treated well, they held a position secondary to their male counterparts. Though there were castes and classes, several instances have been discovered showing marriages between different classes. It is clear that the wealth distribution was quite hierarchical with upper classes engaging in social and artistic living much more than lower classes.

There is no doubt, however, that these Aryans were fierce warriors with intricate weaponry, strong horses, and great military prowess. The Indus Valley civilizations most likely lacked these skills, which ultimately became their downfall. Remember that Aryans were not a united people. Many times they engaged in feuds with many sub-tribes. The Yadu tribe seems to have been the most powerful.

The importance given to the king or the Rajan and emperor or the Samrat is also significant in the Aryan tribes. These kings would engage in sacrificial rituals so as to please the deities. They also had multiple advisors and were expected to govern their people in a moral and just manner. This laid the perfect foundation for an era of massive empires that the subcontinent was to witness in the coming times.

INDIA

CHAPTER 2
THE MAURYAN GLORY

Ancient India's journey into the phase of empires was not a linear one. The evolution of tiny chiefdoms and kingdoms into integrated conquests took centuries to consolidate. The main aspect that distinguished these kingdoms from the empires was not only the expanse of the land conquered but also its ongoing legacy of it. Though these kingdoms would battle each other and the victor would take the territory of the defeated, these territories were not necessarily permanently annexed to the victor's kingdom. While some tribes may have pledged fealty to a powerful king, no significant territorial consolidation came about until around 600 BC when Mauryas built a new political order altogether.

However, before this happened, several powerful kingdoms flourished. The most important ones were Magadha (South Bihar), Vatsa (around Allahabad, now renamed Prayagraj in Uttar Pradesh), Kosala (Oudh, again around Uttar Pradesh), and Avanti (Malwa, Punjab). The story of the expansion of Magadha is the most captivating. Bimbisara and Ajatashatru could arguably be the most powerful of the rulers of this kingdom. They followed a practice of aggressive expansion through conquests and were the primary reason for the growing strength of the Magadhan state.

Then came the Nandas, and this makes for a fascinating story, again. It is said that the last of the successors of Bimbisara's dynasty was Kakavarnin. He was murdered in cold blood with a dagger stabbed in his throat by his own barber. This barber is said to have had an affair with the queen and thus had the ambition of usurping the throne. This barber was none other than the first of the Nanda rulers and was a stern ruler. This first Nanda was responsible for acquiring many kingdoms under him and is considered to have had a significant influence. His successors, however, could not keep up and it is said that the last Nanda ended up being abhorred by his very own subjects. This led to the unavoidable downfall of the Nanda dynasty, which opened the doors for a leader in the form of Chandragupta Maurya to take up the mantle of the emperor.

The Era of Territorial Consolidation

The Mauryan empire was fueled not only by the vacuum created by the hatred towards the Nanda dynasty but by the rapidly changing landscape of the Macedonian conquests in India. In 323 BC, as Alexander, a powerful king from the Macedonian empire, lay on the deathbed, Chandragupta Maurya made the most of this opportunity.

The Mauryan empire flourished between 321 BC and 185 BC and, for the first time in Indian history, consolidated a majority of the subcontinent. Chandragupta Maurya, with the sharp assistance of his advisory minister Kautilya, also called Chanakya, built a model state. Chanakya is famously known for his literary work Arthashastra which is found to be relevant even in this age and times. Arthashastra was the treatise about the model functioning of leadership, government, power, as well as guidelines for economic matters.

Chandragupta Maurya ruled for around 27 years from 324 BC to 297 BC after which his son Bindusara took over. Things continued to be at their peak as the administration went on smoothly. He ruled for another 25 odd years. When Bindusara died in 272 BC, his son Ashoka took over by defeating his brother.

Ashoka was a fierce ruler, rather the most powerful ruler yet. He was known for his violently aggressive conquests and built the biggest empire the subcontinent had ever seen. It stretched even beyond the subcontinent and covered parts of present-day Iran. As glorious as his conquests sound, they were equally cruel. Though he is said to have been trained in martial arts and the aspects of ruling the subjects, his cruelty earned him a bad reputation. The series of his blood-thirsty conquests continued far and wide until the Kalinga War which ended in 261 BC.

This war was fought between Ashoka and Raja Anantha Padmanabha to gain control over Kalinga (around present-day Orissa). This was the only sizable kingdom that had not yet become a part of the Mauryan empire, and this sat like a painful thorn in Ashoka's side. With his massive army of 600,000 soldiers, 9,000 war elephants, and 30,000 cavalries, the enemy, of course, stood no chance; nonetheless, they are said to have fought valiantly.

This war is regarded as the deadliest of all wars with a casualty figure of nearly 250,000. After this war, Ashoka is said to have walked on the battleground, and as he looked at the bloodshed, remorse filled him. This proved to be a turning point not only for the king himself but the entire history of India. With this war ended the age-old tradition of conquests started by Bimbisara, thereby paving the path for a period of relative peace in the country for a little over three and a half decades. This peace was also accompanied by massive religious changes which we shall discuss in the next chapter. But for now, it would suffice to say that this king, whose early life seems to be lost to history, eventually changed its course in a previously never-thought-of manner, with "conquests of religion."

Dhammavijaya vs. Digvijaya

For a long time, it was believed that Ashoka had turned into a Buddhist monk. Now, however, we know that isn't true. He remained a ruler who followed the Buddhist teachings of Dhamma that is peace and tolerance. He swore to conquer by spreading these teachings (Dhammavijaya) rather than conquering territories (Digvijaya). This was one of the biggest influences on the Buddhist movement in India.

Siddhartha's Awakening

Buddhism came into existence around the sixth century BC. It was founded by Siddhartha Gautam also known as Gautam Buddha (meaning the enlightened one). Siddhartha was born in a royal Hindu family in Lumbini (current-day Nepal) in around 623 BC and led quite a protected life. There are disagreements over this date too. It is said that there was a prophecy made at the time of his birth that he would either be a great king or become an ascetic. The legend goes on to talk about how Siddhartha, curious about the world, left the palace and thus became aware of four realities of life that turned his perspective around completely—old age, suffering, death, and ultimate truth. These later became the basis of his teachings.

Buddhism is a religion without deities. It's more a way of life and a set of teachings that guide that way. Buddha went around teaching what he had himself learned from his enlightenment under the Bodhi tree. His followers banded into what came to be known as Sangha. These were groups of his disciples that took on this learning and then went far and wide propagating them further. They lived a simple life, away from attachment to material things.

It has been observed that Buddhism has many principles in common with Hinduism from ancient times. Some theological experts even say that Buddhism is like an off-shoot of Hinduism. But regardless of the commonalities and differences, these teachings began to catch on quickly because of the widespread philosophical changes. As Buddhism had a completely internal focus rather than prescribed external rituals, even people from all socioeconomic classes could partake in it equally. Remember that this was also the time that people were getting tired of constant wars. Thus a religion propagating peace was a perfect fit. And on top of everything it promised them a path to salvation that could be followed in this very life.

Ashoka and His Edicts

In the Mauryan empire, Buddhism had a deep influence. Many families were already practicing Buddhist teachings. When it came to Ashoka, it is clear he converted to Buddhism at some point. But what that point might have been is still unclear. Some believe that it was the bloodshed we spoke of in the last section that led him towards Buddhism. Others have another theory.

Prior to becoming the king, Ashoka had already begun to show the makings of a fierce leader. Thus his father Bindusara sent him to Ujjain as his Governor. Here, Ashoka is said to have fallen in love with the daughter of a merchant, Devi or Vidisha Mahadevi. He never married her but they had two children. This woman is said to have been a Buddhist. The current popular belief is that Ashoka was already a non-practicing Buddhist, taking after his lover when he became king, and thus was heartbroken when he realized how badly he had slaughtered men as well as the Buddhist principles.

After adopting Dhamma in the right sense, he went on to propagate its teachings by engraving it on rocks and pillars. These are known as edicts and were placed throughout the empire. Not only that, he even went on tours himself now and then to spread these teachings and also to understand the pulse of his people. People's welfare was given the highest priority. Along with constructing several hospitals for people and animals, watersheds, rest houses, and other such public welfare projects, he also constructed Stupas and Viharas for the monks. He even sent his son Mahinda and daughter Sanghamitta to Sri Lanka to spread the teachings of Buddhism. It is because of this that Buddhism seems to have been integrated more and more with the common people's lives.

Beginnings of Jainism

The Mauryans, right from Chandragupta Maurya, had intriguing and vibrant religious beliefs. While Ashoka propagated Buddhism, seeds of Jainism had already been planted by the first great Mauryan, Chandragupta Maurya. It is said that Lord Mahavira, the founder of Jainism, often preached to the Mauryas. While some sources say Chandragupta was born to a high-caste Kshatriya family but later converted to Jainism, there are others that portray him as having been a Jain king right from the beginning. Whatever the case may be, it is clear that Mauryans weren't restricted by closed religious boundaries but, on the contrary, have been seen to adopt other religions openly.

Chandragupta was deeply dedicated to his guru Bhadrabahu, a Jain monk. When the monk decided to move to the south because of an impending famine he predicted, Chandragupta also abdicated his throne and moved to Shravanabelagola with his guru. He remained there until his last days.

Though he himself followed Jainism, he did not propagate it on a great scale. This task was later taken up by Samprati, one of Ashoka's grandsons. He is said to have used Jainism as a shield for gaining back some separated territories by sending soldiers as Jain monks. But apart from this, he seems to have been a great patron of Jainism.

CHAPTER 3

THE AGE OF THE GUPTAS

The Mauryan empire began its downhill journey soon after Ashoka's death in 232 BC. The years that followed have often been considered the Dark Ages of India. For almost five centuries the Indian subcontinent bore witness to several foreign invasions including Bactrian, Parthian, and even Turkestani invasions. No Indian king was now formidable enough to live up to the legacy left behind by Ashoka, and the empire that had Pataliputra (present-day Patna) as its bustling capital eventually receded into complete insignificance.

Though "Dark Ages" may sound sinister, it wasn't all bad. This period saw the expansion of artistic and cultural influences. Under Mauryas, there wasn't necessarily much patronage given for arts. Besides Ashoka's edicts, discussed earlier, there wasn't much in the form of great architectural or artistic structures. After the conquests ended, however, there was a boom in literary, artistic, and scientific advances. Patanjali's text on yoga, Manusmriti (code of law given by Manu), and Vatsyayana's Kamasutra all came into existence in the second century BCE; the first play was written by Ashvaghosha who went on to become the mentee of King

Kanishka, yet another powerful king.

The conservative and orthodox mind may consider these advances as secondary to territorial consolidation, but the 400–500 years in between the Mauryas and the Guptas proved to be enlightening. Surprisingly, even Indian rulers engaged in expansion and successfully invaded parts of Central Asia, though not for long. Many kings came and went. The Shungas, Kanvas, Shatavahanas, and the Yavanas (the Indo-Greek invaders) call for a special mention for the campaigns they ran. Their coins and inscriptions provide us with a wealth of information.

The Classical Age

As the age of invasions and experiments passed, the Indian subcontinent finally came into its own with amazing advancements in all fields. The empire flourished between 320 to 550 AD right from parts of southern India, as well as central and northern India. This is known as the classical age especially because of the brilliance achieved in terms of arts, architecture, religion, sciences, and even philosophy. The prosperity and growth attained by the people during this age were particularly remarkable. But interestingly not much is known about the beginnings of this dynasty. However, the travel logs of the Buddhist monks tell us much of what we know.

Another Founder Named Chandragupta

It's a funny coincidence that the course of India's history was changed more than once by a king named Chandragupta, one in 320 BC and the next in 320 AD. Thus, he came to be known as Chandragupta I to avoid confusion. Chandragupta I was not the first of the Gupta rulers but was certainly the first to be recognized for his prowess. The Gupta dynasty seems to have begun with Srigupta, a king of a small kingdom in Magadha and succeeded by his son Ghatotkacha. Chandragupta was

Ghatotkacha's son and was indeed the one to take the Gupta empire to never-before-thought-of heights. He was adorned with the title of Maharajadhiraja, or king of kings, as he expanded his small inheritance of a kingdom into a respectable empire either through conquest or by marriage.

It is believed that Chandragupta I was the first of his dynasty to be cast on the seals of the kingdom. Though the expanse of his kingdom is quite large, right from Ganga in Southern Bihar to Allahabad in Uttar Pradesh, not much is known about how he acquired these territories. It is assumed that most of them may have come to him in his marriage alliance with his Licchavi Queen Kumaradevi.

However, no matter the territory expansion, the Guptas still remained an obscure entity in history until the arrival of Chandragupta's son Samudragupta.

Samudragupta and His Conquests

According to an inscription on a pillar found in Allahabad, written in a script known as Ashoka Brahmi, Samudragupta had succeeded his father not only on the throne but was also the rightful successor to his title of Maharajadhiraja (king of kings). He undertook several campaigns that helped him expand the Gupta kingdom. First, he is said to have headed to present-day Uttar Pradesh and Rajasthan and then down south, defeating several more kings. The core of the Gupta kingdom is said to have been around present-day West Bengal, Uttar Pradesh, Bihar, Madhya Pradesh, and parts of Rajasthan and Punjab. Furthermore, several other rulers in and around the Indian subcontinent are mentioned in the inscription to have asked for Samudragupta's help in their own territorial campaigns while accepting his kingdom as a sovereign one itself. In inscriptions, he is often referred to as the world ruler despite his empire being limited to the Indian subcontinent only.

Samudragupta, and rather all the Gupta rulers, seem to have been quite fond of grand titles as well gestures. And thus, these inscriptions need to be taken with a pinch of salt. Samudragupta particularly is said to have performed the Ashvamedha ritual of a horse sacrifice and even gifted 100,000 cows to his Brahmin followers. He is likely to have had a leaning towards the deity Vishnu and has even been characterized as Vishnu reincarnate due to his "world-ruler" fame.

Though nowhere close to, let's say, Ashoka's empire, Samudragupta had amassed a commendable expanse of territory. While the inscription goes on to describe the greatness of this king with several titles, the Gupta kingdom would never be a pan-India empire. This is mainly because of what some historians consider a flawed political policy. It is often surmised that the reason the Gupta rulers did not expand the empire as much as they could have was this very policy.

The Guptas, it has been found, would battle the kings and even win many of those battles. But they hardly ever annexed these territories to their own kingdom. These kingdoms were only asked to pay some kind of a tribute to the Gupta victors after which the defeated kings were allowed to run their kingdoms as before and the Gupta forces withdrew. On the one hand, this helped the Guptas accumulate massive amounts of wealth which would then be used as patronage for different forms of artistic and cultural projects. But on the other hand, it completely undermined the political hold of the Guptas by reducing battles and conquests only to a manner of exchanging wealth. Rather than territorial consolidation. Of course, for what it's worth this may be considered by some just a clever way of amassing wealth apart from violence and brutal aggression, especially as feudalism was becoming stronger.

But regardless of the policy he followed, Samudragupta also maintained a fierce military. It has been observed by many historians that the Guptas were fantastic adaptors and adapted their military equipment as well as battle styles based on the opponents they faced, specifically the Scythians like Shakas and the Kushanas. Samudragupta is even seen donning a Scythian-inspired costume on his gold coins. The Gupta army had even fashioned camouflage garments made using Bandhani (tie-dye) techniques to be used for tactical advantage.

It must be noted that Samudragupta was not only a great warrior but also a great patron of art and culture. The characteristic classical age is in great parts attributed to his reign and his love for arts. He is said to have been a great musician himself. He has been portrayed as a ruler that gave prime importance to the welfare of his subjects and closely followed the Kautilyan Arthashastra guidelines for running the model state. It may well be said that it was Samudragupta who created a prototype that exhibited a strategy that indeed changed the manner of administration and battle for the coming generations.

Samudragupta was succeeded by Chandragupta II also known as Vikramaditya. It is said that he, Chandragupta II, deposed his older brother Ramagupta and attained the right to the throne. Chandragupta II also followed in his father's footsteps, maintaining the empire created by his father and following the same policies.

Life in the Gupta Empire

Since the Gupta rule has been rightly termed as the "golden age," it would warrant a closer look at the lifestyle led by common people. It appears that even though these were "happy times" there was still a strong economic divide between people.

While there was the richer class that lived in big houses with balconies even, the poorer people lived in thatched mud huts with one room.

When it came to religion, the Guptas like the Mauryans seem to have been quite open. But the hold of Buddhism seemed to be getting weaker during this time. Remember that Hinduism as prescribed in the Vedas had still not reached people in the appropriate manner. What was passed on was majorly the practices of the Aryans who invaded several parts of the country. During the Gupta empire though, the sacrificial and ritualistic practices seem to have driven people away from Aryan imposed religious rites through the ages.

This was the same reason probably that people took on very easily to Buddhism too. But here it would be crucial to mention that even though Buddhism may seem like an easy set of teachings on the surface of it, the teachings do require a deep, constant self-awareness which requires that much dedication too. But in the midst of fulfilling their material needs, they may not have had the time or the mental resources to understand the core doctrines of Buddhism.

And hence local deity practices make a strong comeback. People during the Gupta age had strong Vaishnavite and Shivaite influences. These were still forms of Hinduism but just not as it was practiced in the royal classes. A significant event of this time was that all the Vedic epics that were passed on for generations were now compiled in their final form of literary resources. Thus, the ancient Vedic traditions were now put on record and came under the authority of the Brahmins who were considered to be the learned men.

As this authority grew, the social caste system became more pronounced too. Since the Brahmins were more likely to be the people who read and understood Sanskrit, they came to have a hold over bureaucracy as well as common people. The caste system became much more rigid than it previously was. The caste system that was originally treated as the occupational guideline for smooth functioning now became an imposed, hereditary, unsurpassable restriction passed on over generations.

There were four castes—Brahmins, the learned men, Kshatriyas, the warriors, Vaishyas, the traders, and the merchants, and Shudras, the peasants. There was yet another caste called untouchables who were treated as outcasts and were made to live on the outskirts of the villages so that they would not corrupt the other castes with their impurity. Initially, agriculture was also taken up by the Vaishyas but this changed as time passed by. These castes were initially just occupational groups that ensured all quarters of the society functioned well. People could move between these castes if they felt like it. But this changed during the Gupta age. Though it may not have yet become a social evil in the Gupta period, the seeds for it were certainly sown around this time.

All said and done, though, the Gupta rule is said to have been a time of prosperity and growth like no other. The Guptas had territorial control over rich reserves of iron ore and this could have been the main reason behind their advanced metallurgical techniques. This iron ore was a major component not only in internal use but also in overseas trade. Cities were developed as trading centers and port cities while many others were treated as pilgrimage centers too.

Beautiful temples and monasteries were built across the empire. It must be noted that the famous Nalanda University which would later become a hub for learning was constructed during the Gupta period too. The great poet Kalidasa also lived during these times, though we are not entirely sure of the exact dates. Be it the bold and beautiful erotic sculptures at Khajuraho temples or the paintings at Ajanta caves, they have all been darted back to the patronage of Guptas. Arts, particularly painting, was considered to be a respectable occupation.

Arts and entertainment, however, was not the only accomplishment. This age saw tremendous growth and progress in mathematical, scientific, and medicinal lines thanks to some giants in these fields. Aryabhata was one such name. He was the first mathematician-astronomer-physicist to propose that earth was indeed a sphere rather than a flat surface. His idea of using zero as a figure and even his mention of the relativity of motion have made him immortal even in the modern world of physics and mathematics. Vagbhata was the medical expert who lived during the Gupta times. He is considered to have completed the "great medical trio" who lived in Ancient India—Susruta, a surgeon, and Charaka, a physician. Both these lived much before the Gupta empire but Vagbhata was the one to record his learnings in Ashtanga Samgraha, a compilation of eight different branches of medicine.

The Decline of Guptas

The Gupta empire flourished for around 230 years, leaving

significant imprints of its existence on the rest of the events that were to follow. Be it Chandragupta I, Samudragupta, or Chandragupta II, they all provided the Gupta empire with the needed stability with their decades of rule at a time.

Chandragupta I ruled from 320–330 AD, Samudragupta from 335–375 AD, and Chandragupta Vikramaditya from 375–415 AD. That kind of longevity is bound to contribute to at least some part of the Gupta age stability if not all. Chandragupta II, or Chandragupta Vikramaditya as he was fondly called, was then succeeded by Kumaragupta, who again had a peaceful time ruling the empire because of the solid base created over the past many decades.

And then came Skandagupta, during whose reign things started to unravel for Gupta rule. He had to face the unfortunate rebellion of a particular tribe called Pushyamitra. Skandagupta was, no doubt, successful in snubbing the retaliation but it was obvious that the mutiny had left him politically and financially weak. Before the Guptas could heal from this wound, they faced another brutal strike from the Hunas, or the Huns. Again, Skandagupta was successful in driving back these forces. But both these events had left a large gaping hole in the treasuries of the Gupta empire that they were never able to recover from.

The Gupta empire did not die out soon after though. It went on for a few more years when its last ruler Vishnugupta's reign ended. He had ruled from 540–550 AD. There isn't anything known yet about the immediate successors. But one thing we know for certain is that the Gupta rule had lost its "golden" luster long before it ended.

CHAPTER 4
THE CULTURAL SHIFT

Before we move ahead to the beginnings of the medieval period in Indian history, it is essential to consolidate the mammoth changes that were taken from ancient times into medieval times. This is crucial because it is central to understanding the story of India, the perceptions associated with it, as well as the implications these perceptions may have for understanding present-day India.

Until now, we have looked at specific contributions during specific eras. But now, let's take a moment to understand the bigger picture of what Indian culture looked like and how it eventually shifted, rendering some things completely obscure and making others quite conspicuous.

Dharma and Mythology

The Vedic times, despite the time-lapse, continue to have a strong influence on the mindset of the Indian masses even today. A majority of this influence comes from the mythological legends as well as teachings that are passed down from the Vedic period.

Hindu mythology prophesies four eras, or Yugas—Satya Yuga, Treta Yuga, Dwapara Yuga, and lastly Kali Yuga (which is the predicted end of the world). Lord Vishnu holds a special place in this scheme of things. It is believed that Vishnu has ten avatars or incarnations. Every time the world is taken over by evil, Vishnu takes the form of his incarnation and arrives on the earth to defeat evil. Ram and Krishna are believed to be two of those incarnations that appear in Treta and Dwapara Yugas respectively. The two epics are a tribute paid to these incarnations.

As mentioned before, these mythological stories which were initially passed down were documented as literary sources in their final form during the Gupta age. Ramayana and Mahabharata were two of the greatest epics ever written in ancient India. The validity of these epics is certainly shaky at best. Some believe the incidents to be true while others may think of them as completely fictional. Some others might believe that though the events happened, the writers seem to have taken great artistic liberties in their portrayal. Whichever you may choose to believe, it's crucial to be mindful of the line between mythology and history because, without this distinction, we would be treading very dangerous territory.

The Legend of Ram

Ramayana is an epic containing 24,000 verses by Sage Valmiki. This is said to have been originally composed in the fifth century BCE. Ramayana in itself has had a major influence over the religious beliefs of people and hence it is extremely crucial we understand where it came from. While the narrative is a simple story of the victory of good over evil, it presents a number of layers—political, social, ethical—to be analyzed. It is intriguing how Ramayana, as well as Mahabharata, presents great lessons in Dharma or duty. Ram especially has been portrayed as the virtuous hero who put

Dharma before everything else. Ramayana is more than anything else a story of Dharma, an ideal state of existence, and Ram is an ideal man.

The story goes something like this: Dasharath, the king of Ayodhya is a great king who has three wives. The eldest queen gives birth to Ram, the middle gives birth to twins, Lakshman and Shatrughna, and the youngest one births another son named Bharat. In due course, Ram and Lakshman were sent to accompany sage Vishwamitra to help protect his Ashrama from demons. These demons would desecrate the holy rituals with blood and bones and then kill the people performing the sacrifices. Ram and Lakshman, clever, able, and well-trained warriors as they were, defeated the demons and freed the people of the Ashrama of the continued oppression.

After this, the sage took them to the kingdom of Mithila to let them take part in the Swayamvara. This was an event where the prospective grooms had come together to decide who would be the most worthy to be Princess Sita's husband. Ramayana mentions that the king of Mithila, Janak, had found Sita abandoned in a field and had raised her as his own daughter. In this epic, Sita is said to have been born of earth and not much else is mentioned. Janak had decided that Sita would wed the person that successfully lifted Pinaka, the Great Bow of Shiva.

Several men tried but were unsuccessful in moving it even one inch. The ceremony of Swayamvara had gone on for months and the bow remained in its place. The story goes on to mention that even Ravana, the great villain of this legend, had also attempted to pick up the bow. Being a great devotee of Shiva, he was quite certain he would be able to lift it up without any difficulty. Such was his surprise when he found it a terribly difficult task. He picked it up briefly only to drop it and thus was out of the race for Sita's hand. This is said to have bruised his ego beyond words. After all of this, though, when Ram reached the Swayamvara, he is said to have picked it up with ease, and while pulling the string, he broke the bow into two. Everyone was dumbstruck with his strength and he was thus married to Sita with all festivities.

As Dasharath was getting older, he needed a successor and wished for Ram to sit on the throne. Even all his brothers wished for the same thing. Unfortunately, though, the youngest queen was unhappy as she wished for her own son Bharat to be the king. The hatred in her heart towards Ram was so much that she ordered him to leave Ayodhya and go into exile for 14 years. Dasharath refused but Ram, being the ideal son, had made his decision. Sita and Lakshman followed him into exile for his love.

Ram, Sita, and Lakshman lived the next 14 years in a forest, facing and overcoming many obstacles including dangerous demons along the way. One such demon was Surpanakha, Ravana's sister. Surpanakha is said to have fallen for Ram but being a married man, he told her to talk to Lakshman. Lakshman, making fun of her appearance, refused too. In her fit of anger, she threatened to hurt Sita and in retaliation, Lakshman is said to have shot her nose with an arrow.

In pain, she went to her brother Ravana and all hell broke loose. Ravana saw this as the perfect opportunity to show the world who was more powerful among the two. And thus, he drew a cunning plan to kidnap Sita and thus lure Ram into battle. The story says that Ravana mesmerized Sita with a golden deer outside their hut in the forest. When Ram and Lakshman went to catch the deer at Sita's request, he, Ravana, came in the guise of a hermit. He then took Sita to his kingdom Lanka and imprisoned her there.

Ram, with the help of his great devotee Hanuman, the monkey commander of a monkey army, fought a great battle with Ravana. Ravana is said to have been a great warrior too with many great talents. But his only downfall is said to have been arrogance and ego. After Ram won the battle, he came home with Sita as their exile too had ended. His brother Bharat never ascended the throne, always waiting for his brother to come back.

As things got back to normal, Ram one day heard one of his subjects raise doubts about Sita's purity as he passed by. This kept eating him from within and though he trusted Sita completely, he believed it his duty to dispel all doubts from his subjects' minds. He thus tells Sita to give Agnipariksha, the test of fire, where she would be required to walk through the fire. And since both of them know that she is blameless, she will come out safe and sound. Sita, though terribly hurt, walked through the fire without a scratch on her body. However, after this, rather than returning to the palace, she went into exile once again to live at sage Valmiki's Ashrama. There she gave birth to Ram's two sons, Luv and Kush. After years of exile, Ram found out about his sons and invited them to the palace. But for Sita, he again asked for the same test of sanctity to be proven to his subjects as she had been under the roof of another man all these years. Sita then took the final test and asked the earth to swallow her back to where she came from. The earth shattered open and Sita went away forever.

That is the great Ramayana story. It's not a happy ending but it's certainly one that raises questions as well as answers. Ram's willingness to give up the love of his life solely for the Raj-Dharma, the duty to his kingdom, has been a controversial aspect. But as mentioned before, this is a story of idealism and it delivers exactly what it promises. Also, remember that despite the fantasized elements, the names of the places are quite real. Even many research studies suggest that this might indeed have been inspired by true events.

The Epic of Mahabharata

While Ramayana is a tale of the ideal, Mahabharata is the tale of the real. The characters in this story are flawed much like in real life. This story is about cousins who fought for the right to the throne. This story is much more complex than Ramayana as it weaves in numerous other stories, each with a peculiar philosophical discourse. The epic poem written by Vyasa is 100,000 verses long and composed in the fourth century BCE.

Dhritarashtra, the king of Hastinapura, was married to Gandhari and they both had 100 sons who are called Kauravas, and one daughter. Dhritarashtra's brother Pandu was an excellent warrior who took care of the defense of the state, and after fighting tirelessly, he had retired into the forest with his two wives Kunti and Madri. There he had five sons of his own, collectively known as the Pandavas. When Pandu and Madri died in the forest, Kunti came back to the palace with the five sons, and all 105 princes were trained under their teacher Drona.

During their education, however, enmity started brewing between the two groups. Karn, who was yet another student under Drona and an excellent archer also sided with Duryodhana, the eldest of the Kauravas. As Yudhishtir was the eldest among the 105 princes he inherited the throne. He was also quite popular among the people due to his kind nature—again, always dedicated to Dharma. Duryodhana did not agree to this and he made many attempts on the lives of Kunti and her sons.

The Pandavas went into hiding and survived on the alms given by people. One day they found themselves at the Swayamvar of Draupadi, the beautiful princess of Panchal, seeking alms as usual. The task for the Swayamvar was not easy. There was a pole at the top of which was a fast-spinning fish. The prospective grooms had to shoot the fish by looking at its reflection in the water kept under the pole. No one had been able to make the shot yet, including the Kauravas. Karn was not even given a chance because Draupadi announced that she would not marry someone from an inferior clan. Arjuna, one of the Pandavas, then stepped forward and shot the fish in its eye with five arrows in a single attempt.

Since Arjuna was not the eldest, it was decided that Draupadi would be the common wife to all five Pandavas. As the news of Arjuna's feat traveled, the Pandavas were invited back to Hastinapur and Dhritarashtra decided to divide the kingdom, giving some part to Pandavas and the rest to Kauravas. Though the land given to the Pandavas was barren, they still made it prosper and named it Indraprastha. Jealous of their success, Duryodhana with Uncle Shakuni invited Yudhishtir for a dice game. Shakuni who was to play on Duryodhan's behalf was a skilled player and Yudhishtir lost everything, including his kingdom and wife. Duryodhana even made attempts to disrobe Draupadi in the dice hall full of people. Eventually, Yudhishtir was given the choice to hand over Draupadi or go into a 12-year exile where no one would know who they were. They chose exile.

While on this exile, they came in contact with the king of the Virat kingdom whom they served as servants. It was only when their exile ended did they reveal their Pandava identity. The Virat king then proposed a marriage alliance and Arjuna's son Abhimanyu was married off to the Virat princess. At this point, the battle between Pandavas and Kauravas was unavoidable. Both parties started gathering allies.

The crucial turning point was Krishna coming on to the side of the Pandavas. Krishna was Kunti's brother's son and was thus a cousin to the Pandavas. He was blessed with divine powers and was the greatest strategist. Krishna played the role of Arjuna's charioteer and was largely responsible for the Pandavas' victory despite having much lesser strength in the war.

There are numerous other stories that haven't been touched upon in this context here. But the main difference between the two epics is Ram and Krishna's differences in their approach. While Ram was the ideal one that always followed Dharma, Krishna was the practical one who believed in Karma or the power of action, even if it meant bending the rules here and there. This is particularly important for the philosophical ideology that the epic in particular and Hinduism in general promotes.

Teachings of the Bhagavad Gita

The war at Kurukshetra is said to have raged for 18 whole days. The casualties on both sides were so horrific that this was named Mahabharata, the Great Indian War. The Pandavas won, thanks to Krishna being on their side. But unfortunately, almost all their family is said to have died, including the Kauravas. After this, the Pandavas reigned for almost 36 years with Dharma (duty towards their subjects).

One of the most important outcomes of this war was the recitation of the Bhagavad Gita by Lord Krishna to Arjuna. Literally translated to "the song of the Lord," it is said to have dissipated the guilt and angst in Arjuna's mind about fighting his own brothers. It is one of the most crucial texts of Hinduism and is in widespread use even today. The life lessons from the Gita have been used even in management teams as philosophical rather than religious principles. Moreover, in its translations from Sanskrit to several Indian as well as foreign languages, it has also served as the easiest form of introduction to Hinduism as a philosophical religion to anyone who would be interested.

Though it is now a part of the Mahabharata epic, many historians believe that it wasn't added to the main epic until later. Thus, while the Gita is believed to have been composed in the fourth century BC, the Bhagavad Gita is likely to have been added in the second century BC. Gita, in simple words, is a conversation between the troubled warrior Arjuna and the all-knowing Lord Krishna. Arjuna poses questions and moral dilemmas which Krishna then resolves with his wisdom as well as the basic principles mentioned in the Vedas.

In essence, when Arjuna refuses to take up arms against his brothers and continues to despair about having to kill his brothers, Krishna talks to him about the soul or Atma that lies beyond the cycle of birth and death. Getting attached to anything and anyone in between this and birth and death only increases the suffering of the souls. It is for this reason that one should keep performing his duty (Dharma) without getting attached to the outcome. These expectations and attachment often hold the individual prisoner when they start thinking of "doing" something rather than something that just needs to be done. Krishna thus enlightens Arjuna that the battle must be fought because it is the right thing. It is because of this knowledge that Arjuna goes on to pick up his bow and arrow and the Pandavas eventually win the war.

Philosophical Roots

It must be noted that the philosophical beginnings of Hinduism are not to be attributed to the Gita. Rather the Gita is the compilation of the philosophy mentioned in the Vedas, a summary if you will. Hinduism, before it got muddled with ritualistic practices under the Brahmanical influence, was indeed a set of philosophies, a way of life, rather than an organized religion. It encourages its followers to gain "true knowledge" that will help set them free.

The Hindu philosophy looks at the universe in terms of two entities—Brahman and Atman. Brahman is the ultimate reality, the highest principle in the Universe. It is what we are made of and what we eventually turn into. It is the one thing that binds us all together. Atman, on the other hand, is the fraction of the Brahman that is within our soul. As long as we are caught in the cycle of birth

and death, Atman is prevented from reuniting with Brahman. Once the soul attains salvation or Moksha though, it goes back to the Brahman.

The attachments that we develop through our lifetime mask this ultimate reality and keep us engaged in meaningless matters. Thus, the purpose of life must be to get rid of these illusions of control and gain true knowledge. For this, it is necessary to look inward and discover the power that comes with that knowledge. The only way to attain salvation is through Yoga (the union of body and soul). Four paths of this union have been identified in the Hindu philosophy—Bhakti Yoga (path of devotion), Jnana Yoga (path of knowledge), Karma Yoga (path of action and duty), and Raja Yoga (the royal path of meditation).

It's no secret that these are abstract concepts that may not be easy to grasp for everyone. Top that with being written in Sanskrit and it's obvious why the Brahmins captured most authority.

Culture and Life in Ancient India

Life in ancient India seems to have been strongly driven by their philosophical orientation. They followed what is known as the Ashrama system. Ashramas are places that were built by sages and acted as resting places for travelers along the way. Using the same analogy, in the Ashrama Dharma, these stages are like the resting places you need to live at and nourish your soul, in order to travel ahead. In this system, every individual's life is divided into four stages or four Ashramas—Brahmacharya (the learning/student phase), Grihastha (the householder phase), Vanaprastha (the retirement phase), and lastly Sanyasa (the phase of renunciation). Every individual regardless of their gender, caste, or occupation goes through these phases.

The Hindu philosophy believes that every individual must fulfill four goals in their lifetime—Dharma (duty), Artha (material wealth), Kama (pleasure), and Moksha (salvation). Some may find it contradictory that Hinduism, on one hand, advocates detachment, and on the other, assumes pleasure and wealth as goals of life. But it is intriguing that this philosophy doesn't expect its followers to stick to abstract ideals but shows them a way in which they can move through the worldly phases of life while ultimately aiming for salvation.

This Ashrama Dharma led to the concept of Gurukuls, which were Ashramas where children would be sent during their Brahmachraya phase. It is estimated that in ancient times even girls and children from lower castes were educated in these Gurukuls. But as the Brahmanical, patriarchal influences increased, these educational institutes became reserved only for boys belonging to upper classes.

Once the education was completed, the individual was expected to get married and take up the responsibilities of his family—earn enough money, raise children, and protect his wife.

As his children grew up—sons educated and daughters married off—he then moved into Vanaprastha Ashrama. Here, most men left their homes and retired into forests. They lived off the alms given to them by the people in nearby villages. This was supposed to be the beginning of detachment after having had the opportunity to experience the worldly pleasures of intimacy and attachment.

Last came the Sanyasa phase where the individual would retreat further into the forest and would gradually give up food and sleep in favor of Dhyana or meditation. These people would then take a Samadhi. This would be a state of existence where, while in their physical body, they would still be able to connect to the ultimate reality eliminating the need for physical sustenance eventually.

When we analyze the big ancient Indian picture it is clear that apart from certain evils that were breeding in the murky name of rituals and social order, there was also widespread openness in terms of religious and social beliefs. The Indian philosophy, for the most part, seems to have been "live and let live." However, this was majorly jeopardized when iconoclastic policies followed by the Mughal invasions resulted in a paradigm shift about how religion was viewed.

PART II
MEDIEVAL INDIA

In this part, we explore the period from the 6th century to the 19th century, as one by one great emperor and shrewd explorers invaded the Indian subcontinent to establish legendary empires and to gain supremacy over the exotic Indian treasures.

IV

CHAPTER 5

THE MUGHAL SULTANATE

After the fall of Guptas, the Hun invasions were common but Indian kings like Baladitya, a later Gupta, and Harsha of the Vardhanas successfully defeated them. The latter went on to establish a handsome empire stretched across North India from 606–647 AD. A Chinese traveler by the name of Hiuen Tsang wrote an elaborate account of his visit to Harsha Vardhana's kingdom and its social, economic, and political prosperity. However, Harsha Vardhana had no heirs and after his death, the empire quickly disintegrated into several smaller kingdoms. Interestingly, now the epicenter of the territorial campaigns was shifting to South India and multiple dynasties fought for dominance, Chalukyas and Kadambas leaving an imprint.

Another significant development that was to change the course of not just Indian but global history was the emergence of Islam. The prophet Muhammad was born in 570 AD in Mecca, and when he was around 40 years old, the divine truth was revealed to him. His disciples then traveled around the world with the Arab forces, spreading the message of Islam. The Arab forces soon annihilated the mighty Byzantine empire despite having not much battle experience. The Arab forces progressed with surprising speed and agility, making dents all along the way.

The Arabs invaded Sind in the seventh century and were often called Yavanas, Tajiks, and Turuskas. However, as mentioned earlier, the Indian tradition was so open that the notorious intentions of the Arabs to conquer with monotheistic religious ideas went largely unnoticed. These were merely treated and repelled as isolated invasions rather than a socio-political campaign against the followers of other religious beliefs. Of course, along with ignorance, there was the complacency that eventually led to the downfall of many Indian rulers. Having said that though, the time period between these invasions was characterized by quite peaceful relations between the Arabs and the locals. Whether these were a part of a larger political plan or not, these invasions essentially led the Indian subcontinent into the medieval Mughal era of its maturity.

Babur

Babur was the first Mughal emperor and a descendant of the infamous Genghis Khan as well as Timur. He assumed a position of power quite early in his life at the age of merely 11 years. He ascended the throne of Fergana (present-day Uzbekistan) when his father passed away. His uncles tried relentlessly to dethrone him but this little boy still went on to establish an empire that would rule for centuries in India.

With constant setbacks in battle and mutinies back home, Babur eventually turned his attention away from his state of origin and started moving east in the hopes of finding a kingdom to rule. He believed that due to his descendence from Timur, he was the rightful heir to the Sayyid dynasty led by Khizr Khan. Khizr Khan was initially left in charge by Timur of his feudal acquisition in Punjab. Even with the twisted logic, there was yet another flaw in Babur's plans. The Sayyid dynasty had already been ousted by Ibrahim Lodhi. But Babur was a man on a mission and eventually defeated Ibrahim Lodhi in 1526.

He, thus, became the Sultan of the Sultanate consisting of Delhi and Agra. Lodhi, however, was not the last of Babur's worries. The Indian Rajputs, especially Rana Sanga of Mewar, were putting on a strong front. But when Sanga died, possibly poisoned by one of his own men, Babur's road to consolidation was cleared. He immediately began his expansion strategy with the latest weapons like guns and cannons. This gave him a huge advantage over his enemies.

He was a lover of the arts and showed a deep appreciation of the various Indian structures. He writes about these in his autobiography Baburnama which in itself was a milestone none of the other Mughal emperors had yet achieved. However, this liberalism did not seem to translate to religious figures. He displays blatant anger towards "naked" Jain idols that he ordered be destroyed. Even the Guru Granth Sahib, the holy scripture of Sikhs, written by Guru Nanak, lists a number of brutalities unleashed by Babur on his subjects. But the same scripture goes on to mention that Babur called to meet Guru Nanak after hearing his song. In that conversation, when Guru Nanak stood up to him and advised him to free the prisoners and be a just king, Babur is said to have repented for his sins. The legend even claims that he let the prisoners go and changed his ways. However, mixed his legacy, his name has surely been etched in history.

Humayun

When Babur died after a prolonged illness in 1530, his son Humayun inherited the Mughal empire. The empire stretched over present-day Afghanistan, Pakistan, Northern India, and Bangladesh. Despite the vastness of this empire, Humayun was still battling the ghosts of his father's rule. The Mughals had not yet been accepted by their subjects as their rulers. The battles of Panipat, Khanua, and Ghaghara were some of the fiercest battles fought.

Humayun continued to be challenged too. He was first called into battle in 1535 by Bahadur Shah of Gujarat. Humayun occupied Gujarat but had to fight off Bahadur Shah every now and then. This threat was neutralized only in 1537, but Humayun's worries were far from over and Sher Shah of Sur defeated Humayan twice, first in Chausa in 1539 and later in Kannauj in 1540. This marked the end of Humayun's first stint in India. However, there was more to come. After going back to Iran, he again consolidated a bigger army with the help of Shah Tahmasp and besieged Kandahar in 1545. He then began his march back to India, winning Lahore in 1555 and in a few months securing his place at the throne of Delhi and Agra.

He is said to have been a patron of several long-lasting observatories. He also was responsible for promoting the development of the Safavid style of painting characteristic of the Mughal culture in India. Like his father, his life was also chronicled in a biographical form by his sister Gulbadan Begum. Even his death seems to signify his love for books. He is said to have died by a fatal fall from the staircase of his library when he was coming down, his arms full of books.

Akbar (1556–1605)

Akbar, Humayun's son, inherited the Mughal throne at the almost ripe age of 14. He was thus mentored and advised until he came of age by Bairam Khan, an advisor of the Mughals. Akbar is hailed by most as an able and ambitious leader. He undertook multiple campaigns and made special efforts to transform the meager kingdom left to him by his father. He didn't merely conquer territories but ensured that his subjects were also loyal to him. He revised the tax structure so as to put no added financial pressures on non-Muslims. He even reduced the "tribute taxes" levied on the Rajput kings. The result of this was that Akbar was spending less time putting out fires all over the place and more time strategizing, administering, and executing.

Akbar also expanded the empire through marriage alliances regardless of religion. Though it was a common practice to marry the Hindu princesses to Muslim conquerors, this was often done as a means of humiliating the Hindu royal class into submission. However, when Akbar married Jodha Bai, a Rajput princess, the men in her family were made members of his royal court, the same as his Muslim in-laws. This earned him loyalty and respect amongst his allies. Of course, it is not unimaginable that some people were against this kind of integration.

Akbar was a truly multicultural emperor. He is said to have built within Fatehpur Sikri (the walled city with Persian architecture that he had designed) a temple or Ibadat Khana where he frequently met with learned men from other religions. He even allowed the construction of a church in Agra during his time. He is also associated with a faith he himself established called Din-i-Ilahi which combined elements from Islam, Hinduism, and Zoroastrianism. However, this never caught on. Regardless, he himself expressed openness and tolerance towards all religions, even participating in festivals of other faiths.

Akbar was not an artist himself but this never stopped him from appreciating art and talent whenever he saw it. He is well-known for his patronage of the Navratnas, or the nine gems in his court—Abul Fazl, the biographer and author of Akbarnama, Abul Faizi, a scholar, Tansen, a singer, Raja Birbal, the witty advisor, Raja Man Singh, the lieutenant, Abdul Rahim Khan-I-Khana, a poet, and Fagir Aziao-Din and Mulla Do Piaza, two more advisors.

Some historians believe that Jahangir may have poisoned his own father so as to gain control of the powerful throne.

Jahangir (1605–1627)

It is said that when Akbar died, Jahangir's son Khusrau Mirza was considered for the position. However, Jahangir took over instead and began ruling within a few days of Akbar's death. On most accounts, he seemed to have an ambitious attitude, similar to his father. Though Akbar had expanded the Mughal empire, there were pockets within that empire that had not yet pledged allegiance to the Mughals, such as the Mewar province. One of Jahangir's greatest victories was the resolution of this conflict.

It is said that Jahangir had many wives, some say close to 20. These were marriages for the purposes of alliances with the Rajputs. In 1611, he is said to have married Mehr-un-Nisa who he later named Nur Jahan. Nur Jahan was a beautiful, smart, strong woman well-trained in the art of war. She was known to have a strong influence over Jahangir's court matters as well as to have led the army into the battlefield.

As for Jahangir's views on religion, he seems to have had an ambiguous stance. While he didn't exact any additional taxes from non-Muslims or even give any special powers to Muslims in his court, he also showcased instances of specific hate crimes towards some Hindus and Sikhs. For example, he executed the Fifth Sikh Guru, Guru Arjan Dev, resulting in friction between Muslims and Sikhs. He is also said to have tortured Hindu men for marrying Muslim girls in Kashmir. This suggests that he agreed with interfaith marriages only as long as they resulted in conversion to Islam.

After Jahangir passed away, Nur Jahan took up the mantle of the emperor. Well, almost. When she started issuing royal mandates in her name, Jahangir's son Khurram, who would later be called Shah Jahan, imprisoned her for the rest of her days.

Shah-Jahan (1628–1658)

Legend has it that even though Akbar's first wife didn't have any children of her own, she was told by a psychic that she would still raise a future Sultan, and Akbar had the intuition that Khurram, Jahangir's third son, would be that future Sultan. This resulted in a strong bond between Akbar and Khurram. In 1607, he was engaged to Arjumand Banu Begum. However, their marriage was halted due to, again, a prediction made by the fortune teller. In the meantime, he was married off to two other princesses for the purpose of political alliances. He had one son each with those wives. But it is said that his heart remained with Arjumand Banu. When they got married, they went on to birth 14 children, seven of whom made it to adulthood.

Shah Jahan had already proved his mettle as a leader and warrior. He followed an expansion policy in a steadfast manner. While he aligned himself with some Rajput kings such as those of Mewar and Bundelkhand, he took it upon himself to destroy the others like the Rajputs from Bundela. He also involved his son Aurangzeb in his military operations in South India, and the boundaries of the empire widened to include Golconda and Bijapur.

Despite all the military success, one would have to admit that Shah Jahan's most important contribution to history is his larger-than-life tribute to his wife Mumtaz—the Taj Mahal. Even today, people flock to Agra to bear witness to the beauty of this white marble monument. But that wasn't the only thing he had built. Red Fort and Jama Masjid in New Delhi and Shalimar Gardens in Lahore are only a couple of the many structures he commissioned.

When Mumtaz died after birthing her 14th child, Shah Jahan was shattered. It is said that he isolated himself for almost a year. When he did emerge at the behest of one of his daughters, his hair had gone gray beyond measure at the early age of 40.

He went on to rule until 1658 when he fell ill. One of his sons, Dara Shikoh, took up his duties while he recovered. His other son Aurangzeb had different plans. He was furious that he wasn't called upon for assuming the emperor's role. Having been Shah Jahan's governor, he was already skilled at warfare and had an army at hand. He marched on to defeat Dara Shikoh and won. He then went on to imprison Shah Jahan until he breathed his last in 1666.

Aurangzeb (1658–1707)

Aurangzeb is likely the most hated Mughal king in Indian history. He imposed increasingly puritanical practices which were the hallmark of a religious fanatic. Some historians prefer to look at Aurangzeb's reign as divided into two parts. In the first part, between 1658 to about 1680, Aurangzeb was viewed as a skilled and vicious ruler, never loved but respected and feared all the same. During this time, he was observed to be busy protecting his borders from Persians and Turks. A hint of complacency is visible in the manner in which he dealt with Shivaji, the chief of the Maratha kingdom. Aurangzeb didn't know it yet but this chief was to be a large part of the decline of the Mughal empire.

Somewhere around 1680, one can see a clear shift in Aurangzeb's attitude when he started practicing bigotry with his subjects. The poll taxes on non-Muslims which were abolished by Akbar were brought back and tolerance had been wiped clean from the Mughal empire. He even imposed the Islamic Sharia law on the entire empire. This became the major cause for dissatisfaction and even hatred amongst his non-Muslim subjects who were still in a majority throughout the empire. The mutinies and the uprisings that began with the Marathas soon caught up with the Rajputs as well as the Sikhs, but the Marathas still remained Aurangzeb's biggest worry. Even after the dissipation of the Maratha kingdom, the Maratha soldiers that were left behind employed guerilla warfare to disturb Aurangzeb's peace. This worked wonders as even towards the end of his rule he was obsessed with catching up to the Marathas.

Maratha Wars and the Decline of the Mughal Empire

While Aurangzeb was the wealthiest and the most powerful Mughal ruler of all, he also was the reason that the empire was eventually razed to the ground. As mentioned above, Marathas were his most formidable opponents yet, especially under the able and inspiring leadership of Shivaji. Aurangzeb hoped to employ Akbar's old technique with the Marathas—conquer and reconcile. However, this would not succeed with Shivaji. Shivaji had already humbled the likes of Shaista Khan by cutting off his fingers at the Lal Mahal in Pune.

In 1666, Shivaji was invited, rather summoned to Agra to be forced into negotiation and eventually submission. He was to be kept under house arrest until he gave in. But Shivaji made a supremely clever escape and left Aurangzeb fuming. This game of cat and mouse continued with not only Shivaji but all of the Maratha descendants. Aurangzeb had poured so much of the Mughal treasury into these small battles that it had left the Mughal empire quite hollow from within.

Aurangzeb is considered to be the last of the effective monarchs who held the vast empire under them. He had, after all, ruled for 49 years. But unfortunately, his extremist policies had already done permanent damage and it would be impossible for his son and successor Bahadur Shah I to repair any of what was shattered. The massive Mughal empire collapsed in the 18th century and its legacy went down with it.

CHAPTER 6
THE EAST INDIAN COMPANY

Towards the end of the 16th century, the British crown was in desperate need of money and it had found the perfect solution to resolve all their financial concerns. They were to set up trading posts in the East Indies as they called it and gain access to valuable exotic items like spices, metals, tobacco, and so on. Not only that, they would then grant access to only certain traders to trade in that area, exacting some fees and commissions from them too. Overseas travel was a risky business after all. So, the traders preferred to reduce the competition as much as possible.

This idea came to life on December 31st, 1600 when Queen Elizabeth I, with an official charter, granted one group of merchants exclusive trading rights in India. This group of merchants called themselves the East India Company. However, it didn't take much to understand that this was to be the front behind which British imperialism would creep into the Indian subcontinent.

However, Britain was not the first to see an opportunity. Spanish and Portuguese traders had already established their own trading posts, and the British Crown was somewhat paranoid that this could be the determining factor for their power politics. Even they themselves couldn't have imagined how valuable the East Indian Company (EIC) would be in their colonial strategy.

The EIC was founded by two merchants, John Watts and George White. It made its first voyage to India under the command of Sir James Lancaster. The company at this time was still exploring its options for establishing a base for its operations. After the Battle of Swally in 1612 with the Portuguese in Surat, India seemed to be a more and more feasible and profitable prospect. By this time, they had already built their first factory in Masulipatnam in Andhra Pradesh, with the next to come up in 1613 in Surat.

During the time of this development, a large part of the Indian subcontinent was being ruled by Jahangir. The EIC officials were at first viewed as mere supplicants who wanted to establish favorable trading relations. The trading relations would be important, at least in the beginning, especially because the South-East Asian market had already proved difficult for the EIC, due to the strong influence of the Dutch East India Company. Now the EIC traders knew that they would require all the support they could from the local powers. For the first few initial journeys, the Company raised its joint stock separately. This only meant that the risks of the voyage, as well as the ownership of the Company, were shared between different stakeholders. However, after 1657 a permanent joint stock was raised, indicating it was in India for the long haul.

An Era of Exploitation

Corruption and ruthless profiteering seem to have been breeding in the Company from the very beginning. Though the Crown gave an exclusive trading monopoly to the EIC, the Company would still go on to allow its voyagers private trading. This was done under the pretense of giving them added incentives so they would make the dangerous voyage to India. This marked the beginning of conniving exchanges under the flag of the EIC.

It has been noted by many historians that the Company was becoming an increasingly well-oiled exploitative machine with its official company trades and unofficial private trades making a fortune at the cost of the Indian locals. However, this was only the first step. With the passing years, the company's involvement with the Indian subcontinent increased.

The first Company ambassador, Thomas Roe, approached Jahangir in 1612 for permission to reside and build factories in Surat. Jahangir's fascination with European rarities seems to have made the task much easier. The traders now knew that they had a safe path to more authority only if they provided the rulers with something of value in return. With the simple ruse of ingratiating the rulers, the Company officials secured several favors like the abolition of the custom duties. This meant that the Company could engage in unlimited trade of exotic materials without the fear of retribution. The worst part was unlike the previous rulers who spent what they earned in the subcontinent itself, a new order was in the making where the wealth from India was headed straight to the Crown.

Most of the 17th century passed in trading ruthlessly in Indian goods, battling the influence of Dutch East India Company, and also eventually warring with elements of the Mughal empire, particularly Shaista Khan, only to lose and pay fines to Aurangzeb. But while all of this was happening, there were also important developments happening back in Britain. The traders who had amassed infinite fortunes had now gone back to England and created a political climate that gave massive advantage to British trade. By the 18th century, specifically after the Battle of Plassey in 1757, the East India Company established itself as a formidable army rather than a trading company. The battle was fought in the village of Palashi, in Maharashtra. The defeat of Bengal Nawab Siraj-ud-Daula marked the beginning of formal British rule in India.

The Fall of the Honorable Company

The Battle of Plassey gave the British administrators infinite powers over the local functioning. They could now make their own rules for trade and even exact taxes as they saw fit. These were the two biggest forms of revenue for the British Crown. From there the British rule only grew from strength to strength. However, the same could not be said for the Company's future. Back in the British Parliament, there seemed to be a heated debate over the running of the EIC in India and the foul practices it engaged in. Rampant corruption among officials kept surfacing. The first Governor-General of Bengal, Warren Hastings, was even tried for misconduct and demands were made that he should be impeached. Ultimately, he was acquitted but the cracks were openly visible.

The final straw came a few decades later when the "Honorable" Company, as it was so often called, engaged in quite a dishonorable act of leveraging illegal drugs. China was quite famous for its tea which is exported for silver. But the Crown's silver reserves were virtually non-existent. Thus, the Company traders used the illicit production of opium in India and traded it in exchange for

Chinese tea. Opium, being a banned substance in China, triggered "the Opium Wars" between China and the British traders. The first war was fought between 1839 and 1842 while the second one was between 1856–1860.

Better weaponry gave the British an easy win but exposed the cruel intentions of these traders. The fact that the Chinese were coerced into legalizing the opium trade and that the Indian laborers were enslaved for opium production did not sit well with the British Parliament. To add to the list of cruelties, it came to the fore that the EIC had slaughtered those who protested against such brutal slavery in the Indian Mutiny of 1857. The British Parliament refused to renew their contracts and thus the EIC was disbanded in 1858.

The Uprising of 1857

The Indian Mutiny, sometimes also known as the Sepoy Mutiny, broke out in 1857. This was the first-ever widespread resistance to British advances. Though it bore no success, it sent the message to the British Government that the Indian subjects were certainly not as mute and meek as they had expected. The EIC with its unethical practices and oppressive policies had had it coming a long time. A score of different factors impacted this—the social conditions, the oppressive taxation structure, discrimination of Indian soldiers, and so on.

The spark that lit the Company on fire was the use of greased cartridges. There was a rumor that the grease used in cartridges was made from the fats of cows and pigs. To load these, the soldiers had to bite off the ends of the cartridges. This violated both the Hindus and Muslims in whose respective religions consumption of cows and pigs was a sin. Sepoy Mangal Pandey was the first to refuse to use these cartridges and attacked the senior officials. He was hanged on the 8th of April that year.

The fire had been lit. After Pandey, there were several more soldiers from Meerut who refused to use the cartridge too. They were also subjected to long and harsh prison sentences. The Indian soldiers had now had enough. They rebelled by shooting several British officials on May 10th and then marched to Delhi to nominate the frail Mughal king Bahadur Shah II as their ruler. This pattern of revolution followed throughout the northern stretch of the country resulting in fatal consequences for the British officials as well as their families. Only a handful of rulers like Nana Sahib, Rani Lakshmibai, and General Bakht Khan took part in the mutiny while other princes held their silence. The violence reached a point where the British officials took brutal action against the soldiers on mere suspicion even when no violent advances were made. The British engaged in planned and despicable vengeance, far more than the acts of the soldiers had warranted. Eventually, peace was declared in July 1859.

The British Parliament realized that it would be impossible to keep matters running smoothly as before with the same administrators. An extensive house cleaning exercise was undertaken and thus the decision to disband the East India Company.

The British Raj

The Indian Mutiny was significant for several reasons. One, it led to major structural changes in the British administration. Two, it led the British rulers to engage in a method of policy-making that would require more participation from their Indian subjects. And three, it led to the complete collapse of the traditional monarch-subject relationship that had existed for several centuries in India. While most of the princes stood as the silent spectators to the mutiny, a new realization had dawned on the laypeople that the kings would not be their saviors, rather it was upon their shoulders to save their nations from the plundering foreigners. This realization was also due to the emerging "middle class" from the influence of the Western class system.

It is clear that the first two results mentioned above were more of face-saving strategies to pacify the Indians. But what the British didn't realize was that when combined with the third factor, it would prove to be a fatal blend for their imperialism. The seeds of nationalism had been sown and over the next 90 years or so these seeds grew into a massive tree. The British Raj continued in India from 1858 to 1947, until independence. Volumes of information can be written about this period alone.

The British administration now followed a policy of non-interference in religious as well as royal matters. The princes were appeased by giving them the "freedom" to choose their successors—as long as they pledged allegiance to the British Crown. The Christian missionaries were required to stop proselytizing. This was not due to a change of heart but a fear that protests may break out again.

The British rule in India continued to harness all its power and wealth from three sources—the taxes levied on agricultural yield, the opium trade with China, and the taxes on salt. As the British population of officials and their families in the country increased, hospitals and educational institutes began appearing too. A great contribution of the British to Indian history was the laying of nationwide railroads. Efforts were made, at least on the surface, to integrate the Indian population within the British ranks. Discrimination was nowhere close to ending but the British were putting up a solid front.

PART III
MODERN INDIA

Here we look at the developments of the 20th century and India's march into a new phase of peace and protests. We understand the tough path towards freedom in all its intricacy.

CHAPTER 7
THE FIGHT FOR FREEDOM

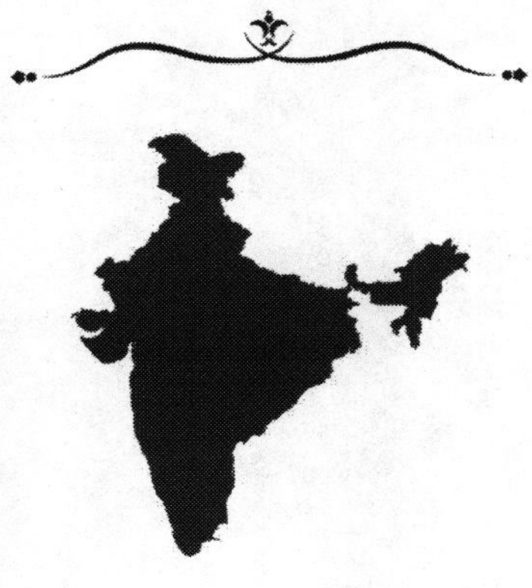

The Nationalist Movement in India took root in 1885 when the Indian National Congress (INC) held its first convention. Founded by a civil servant named A.O. Hume, it was attended by several Indians who were educated in the British tradition like Dadabhai Naoroji, Romesh Chunder Dutt, Surendranth Bannerjee, and so on. The initial Congressman demanded representation in the British administration. Dadabhai Naoroji even went on to be elected as a member of the British House of Commons. They sought the path of dialog and deliberation with the British regarding the policies so as to come to those that would be best for their fellow Indians. The INC was to become the party that possessed a strong influence throughout the freedom struggle.

Although, there were others who did not quite agree. Bal Gangadhar Tilak was the first to sound out the call of Swaraj, or self-rule. He was of the opinion that colonial education was doing a disservice to Indian culture and should therefore be renounced completely. He and other followers of this school of thought believed that there could be no compromise. They declared that Indians were capable of governing themselves and that the British would have to leave for India to be truly independent.

These two schools of thought continued to have clashes all through the freedom struggle. It was observed that more and more people were becoming radicalized due to the continued oppression of their fellow countrymen by British officials. The Swadeshi Movement (1903–1908) in response to the administrative decision to partition Bengal proved that Indians were now standing up to the imperial powers. Tilak was arrested for his radical views and sentenced to six years imprisonment in Mandalay, Burma. After his release in 1914, he, along with Annie Besant, would lead the Home Rule Movement which lasted between 1916–1918. The freedom struggle had begun and the people would settle for nothing less.

Gandhi and His Mass Appeal

Mohandas Karamchand Gandhi, fondly known as Mahatma Gandhi, has been one of the biggest influences

on the struggle for independence. Until he arrived on the scene, there were only two ways to respond to the British: fight or compromise. He brought in the third and, in its own way, most revolutionary response—Satyagraha, or non-violent resistance. There are, of course, multiple perceptions regarding his style of leadership, and he may even be considered a pacifist by right-wing thinkers. But whatever the disagreements may be regarding his style, no one can deny the fact that here was a man who had brought people together like no one else ever before. Followers were drawn to him regardless of their religion, caste, and creed, and all the freedom struggle needed at the time was a leader like this at the helm steering the diverse ship.

After having been a victim of racism and discrimination in South Africa, Gandhi decided to dedicate himself to the freedom struggle. Many have called Gandhi's legacy out for being a racist himself but the fact that he did lead India head-first into a new phase of the fight for independence cannot be erased. His first foray into this movement was when the British Government passed the Rowlatt Act of 1919 permitting the officials to detain indefinitely and sentence the accused without a trial. This enraged Gandhi and he thus called an Anti-Rowlatt Satyagraha. This would mean that people would engage in peaceful meetings. The Government came down hard on these resulting in violence all over.

Jallianwala Bagh Massacre

Millions rose up to Gandhi's call and organized peaceful protests. In Punjab, two leaders were arrested for such protests, Dr. Saifuddin Ketchlew and Dr. Satya Pal. Discontent was evident among people. A week later, thousands of people gathered again in Jallianwala Bagh, peacefully protesting the arrests of their leaders. The British authorities decided to thwart these protests again. One General Dyer reached the grounds where the meeting was in progress. He ordered the only exit be shut off, and then opened fire. It was raining bullets as men, women, and children screamed in agony. But such was the anger against the government that rather than die from Dyer's bullet, they chose to kill themselves by jumping off in a well that was on the ground. More than 2,000 were massacred that day, and this was one of the turning points that was to shape the ideas of many of the revolutionaries in the future. This was also the time when Gandhi concluded that complete independence was the only way things would change.

The Non-Cooperation Movement

This was the first mass movement headed by Gandhi. After Jallianwala Bagh, Gandhi realized that it would not be enough to only tell the government that there was disagreement but there would need to be sufficient impact. Thus, he called on all Indians to stop going to work and to stop using products that were not made in India. Gandhi, with a Charkha (a device to spin yarn), is a common image in the historic symbology of modern India. He made his own Khaki clothes and urged people to do the same.

Beginning in 1920, this movement incorporated men, women, and kids and gained massively from this all-around contribution and participation. They now had the option to fight for freedom with something routine that they could do rather than something huge and heroic. The only instruction they had to follow was Ahimsa, or non-violence.

The movement went on for two years and was becoming a bigger worry by the day for the British. Unfortunately, however, the non-violent movement turned violent as a group of extremists burned down a police station in 1922 in Chauri Chaura, Uttar Pradesh. Several policemen were killed and Gandhi called off the movement completely. Gandhi was then arrested on the charge of sedition and imprisoned for six years.

After this, many people broke off from Gandhi, unhappy with his unilateral decision to call off the movement because of one incident. Many even thought that he did it so he wouldn't have to take the blame for the Chauri Chaura violence.

The Revolutionary Called Bhagat Singh

Bhagat Singh was born on September 28th, 1907, and grew up in an environment of political awareness and debate. He was an articulate man and frequently wrote for publications in his college. He was an atheist who found himself drawn to Marx's ideas of communism. It was no surprise that he did not align with the Gandhian philosophy of non-violence. Not that he advocated violence, but he did believe that sometimes resorting to violence may be the only option there was. It was because of his radical ideas that he got on the British officials' radar. He was arrested once on the suspicion of his involvement in a bomb explosion but then released on bail.

When the Simon Commission was set up in 1928, Indians reacted with tremendous anger. This commission was set up to review the Government of India Act of 1919. This act was originally passed with the intent of getting more Indians to participate in the Government. This was to be in effect for ten years. Ironically, though, the commission set to review it had no Indian representation at all which eventually led to the boycott of the Simon Commission. On its arrival, it was met with black flags and the protest was led by a senior leader of the independence movement known as Lala Lajpat Rai. Though the crowd was completely peaceful, the British reacted with brutal force opening a lathi charge. Rai was severely injured along with many others. Eventually, Rai succumbed to his injuries, further aggravating the others.

Bhagat Singh and Chandrashekar Azad, another revolutionary, decided to avenge Rai's death. They planned to assassinate James Scott who had ordered the lathi charge. They carried out the assassination as planned but in the case of mistaken identity had killed John Saunders. The killing was condemned by all but Bhagat Singh managed to escape.

However, in 1929, Bhagat Singh, along with his friend Sukhdev decided to detonate a bomb in the Chamber of Deputies, Paris, and turn themselves in because they wanted a trial. They wished for the people to hear all they had to say. The bomb was harmless but injured a few people. Bhagat

Singh and Sukhdev had plenty of opportunities to escape but chose not to, and remained in place shouting "Inquilab Zindabad," or "Long Live Revolution!" He was charged with terrorism and eventually hanged on March 23rd, 1931.

Bhagat Singh knew very well what was in store for him and yet he chose to go that path because he wanted to express his ideology. He was of the opinion that you can kill a person but not ideologies.

Civil Disobedience Movement

Gandhi began this movement in 1930 a little after he was released from jail. After the earlier non-cooperation movement, this time it was intended to be a notch higher. This time the movement was to break certain laws in a peaceful manner. Gandhi would march from Sabarmati Ashram in Gujarat to Dandi to oppose the ridiculous taxation structure of the British. He and his followers marched almost 390 kilometers for 25 days. The people of India were burdened with very high salt taxes and this was impacting people at the very grass-roots level. Thus, Gandhi marched all the way to Dandi shore, and on April 6th, 1930 he held out the salt on the shores in his hand. Thus began the civil disobedience movement. But salt was only a part of it. Girls and women picketed liquor shops and opium trading dens. In some states, entire villages refused to pay "protection taxes" to the local guards. In short, taxation was boycotted on a large scale.

Gandhi was imprisoned again on May 5th, 1930 and the nation turned upset and violent. The Government in turn kept getting more and more repressive which did not help the situation. The Purna Swaraj (complete independence) slogan was now ripe with excitement.

Gandhi-Irwin Pact

Gandhi was released in January 1931. The then Viceroy of

India, Lord Irwin, had a fair grasp of the influence Gandhi exercised over people. As the movement gained more steam, he offered to negotiate with Gandhi the terms of the truce, of sorts. Hopeful and optimistic as he was, Gandhi agreed and called for ending the movement. This angered many people because the movement that was turning successful was being called off only on the back of a possibility. People felt disillusioned and disappointed.

The Gandhi-Irwin Pact was signed in 1931 which said that in return for ending the civil disobedience, India would be allowed to participate in the Second Round Table Conference, all political leaders would be released (except for terrorists like Bhagat Singh who was in prison at the time waiting for his death sentence), and the coastal people would be allowed to make salt for personal consumption.

Gandhi was saddened by Bhagat Singh's sentence even though he did not agree with his methods. He did whatever he could to try to save him from being executed. He wrote a fervent letter to Irwin who was also his friend. Even Irwin requested the British judge to reassess the situation. But the British Raj was in turmoil as people were finding their voice and raising it fearlessly. The British administration considered it an opportune time to make an example out of the three young revolutionaries.

Freedom, At Last

The Indian sentiment kept getting more and more intense. Unfortunately for the British, as World War II raged at a global level, Civil Disobedience was taken to a whole new level where Gandhi encouraged people to refuse to be part of the war under the British flag. Since the war was fought for the basic democratic rights of citizens, Gandhi reasoned that Indians had no place in the war. The Quit India Movement was initiated in August 1942. Gandhi called on his fellow countrymen to "do or die" and demanded that British forces withdraw from India completely. More arrests followed.

On the world stage, Britain had been drained of resources. And the struggle for independence in India was stronger than ever. To add to the misfortunes of the British Empire, there was also an insurgency in their Balochistan colony, further depleting their resources. Despite the travesties it faced, the British refused to give in to the demands of the Indian leaders. The Quit India Movement was squashed on the basis of the notion that no independence could be granted during a war. The arrested leaders were kept in complete isolation with no news of the world reaching them. Gandhi, because of his depleting health resources, was released from prison in 1944. The other leaders would only be released much later. The gloomy burden of yet another failed movement was weighing down on many.

But around the same time, in 1945, the Labour Party was elected to power. Clement Attlee became the Prime Minister. Attlee had been a part of the Simon Commission back in the day and advocated India's right to self-governance. Finally, preparations were afoot for India to be free.

CHAPTER 8
THE CASUALTY OF PARTITION

The almost 200-year-old British-Indian connection was to be severed. On February 20th, 1947, Attlee made the announcement. The British would finally be leaving the country leaving the Indians to govern themselves all on their own. Attlee ordered Lord Mountbatten, India's last Viceroy, to draw up a plan for the transfer of power.

In May 1947, Mountbatten came up with what came to be known as the Dickie Bird Plan or the Balkan Plan. Here he suggested a constituent assembly that would be joined by the provinces that preferred it. However, Jawaharlal Nehru, an influential member of Congress, was strongly opposed to this idea. He was sure that this would lead to the fragmentation of the princely states into tiny states. Hence the name Balkan Plan stood for Balkanization.

Mountbatten, thus, proposed another plan. This is known as the Mountbatten Plan and includes clauses for the formation of two states. Both states would have the right to formulate their own constitution and would have complete control over the matters of their respective states. The proposed plan was accepted by the Muslim League as well as Congress. There was one more provision that would impact these two nations as well as that of their citizens for years to come. The princely states were given the choice to stay independent or to join either of the two countries.

Two Nation Theory

By the time the Mountbatten Plan was announced, the news of partition was an accepted reality. Some stalwarts like Sardar Vallabh Bhai Patel had given in while some like Muhammad Ali Jinnah were rooting for it. Gandhi and Abdul Ghaffar Khan were the only two left in complete opposition to this plan. But what's interesting is that even that was not the beginning of this so-called Pakistan Movement.

Many people believe that the underlying cause for partition was the core differences in the lifestyles and culture of Hindus and Muslims. People may think that there is so much history between these two, thanks to the Mughal emperors, that it would be impossible for them both to coexist. Well, there is some truth to that statement. There is indeed great history between the two. We have looked at it throughout this book. And we know that it's not all bad history. Sure, Mughal tyrants like Aurangzeb were cruel to their Hindu subjects, but when we look at Mughal history, he seems to be rather an exception than the rule. History is full of evidence that these two religions could have existed peacefully, even lovingly.

Therefore, one may say that it wasn't the fundamental differences between the two faiths that sowed the seeds of insecurity among the two but the British administration itself. After the Indian mutiny, the British carried the fear of protests almost until their rule ended. This is quite apparent in the divide and rule strategy employed by the administration under Lord Dufferin. Though he had permitted the formation of the Indian National Congress, he soon realized the power it could wield. As members started seeking more ways of participation Lord Dufferin steadily grew uncomfortable. He first tried approaching Congress directly requesting the members to keep their discussion limited to "non-political social reforms." When Congress refused he even reached out to the elite patrons of INC and tried to convince them to withdraw their patronage. When that didn't work he prohibited government officials from participating in the INC meetings.

Around the same time, he reached out to certain British loyalists in the Indian community. One of these people was Sir Syed Ahmad Khan. He was the same person who had pushed for Western, scientific education for Muslims in India. And thus began the speeches that would play upon people's insecurities. Syed Ahmad Khan was the first to speak about the two-nation theory in these speeches. The result was that by the early 1900s a section of the society firmly believed in the idea of a separate nation for Muslims. And thus was formed the All India Muslim League in 1906.

The All India Muslim League demanded that separate electorates be granted for Muslims where only the Muslims could be candidates for certain seats and only Muslims could vote for these. This demand was approved through Morley Minto Reforms or the Indian Council Act of 1909. This was the first outright communal administration passed by the government. This eventually led to a section of Hindus feeling paranoid, and thus organizations like Rashtriya Swayamsevak Sangh (RSS) and the Akhil Bharatiya Hindu Mahasabha came into existence.

It's interesting to note that Muhammad Ali Jinnah who

was a strong advocate of the need for a separate Muslim state in later years never supported these divisive moves. It's only later, possibly due to the cumulative effect of his life circumstances such as disagreements with Gandhi and the strong influence of Islamic extremists like poet Iqbal Khan, he eventually changed his mind. He wouldn't let the idea of Pakistan go even when Gandhi and Nehru offered him the position of Prime Minister of the independent state.

The Partition

The Indian Independence Act of 1947 received royal assent on July 8th, 1947 and it would be in effect from August 15th, 1947. This would be a joyous celebration if it wasn't marred by the pain and horror of Partition. About five weeks prior to the British departure from India, a lawyer, Sir Cyril Radcliffe, was hastily sent in. He arrived on July 8th, 1947, and was ordered to draw the line that would determine the fate of these two countries for a long time to come. For someone who had no understanding of the people or the place, this was an impossible task. Yet, Radcliffe drew a line, the "Bloody Line" as it is often called.

Dividing a multicultural nation like India on the basis of religion could not have been an easy task. States like Punjab and Bengal for instance had both massive Hindu and Muslim populations with neither in a clear majority. Another major problem was posed by the princely states which covered nearly 48% of the Indian territory (Pal, 2017). These could not be partitioned as they weren't under British occupation. So, they would be given the choice to stay independent or to join one of the two countries.

Ultimately, a bizarre line was drawn that seemed to travel through people's homes and hearts alike. For instance, the two holy sites of the Sikhs, some fifty-odd kilometers apart, were now in two different countries. Eastern and Western extremities of India were determined to be territories of Pakistan which formed Eastern Pakistan (later formed into a separate nation of Bangladesh) and Western Pakistan. The partition was followed by a mass exodus as millions of Hindus, Muslims, and Sikhs were made to leave their homes and travel to the nation where they supposedly belonged. Riots ensued as children were slaughtered and women raped to prove the superiority of the perpetrators' religion, whatever it may be. The people of the two countries still feel the pain as memories come rushing and there are still families that live right across the border and have hardly seen each other.

The Republic of India

Partition had left a scar in India's freedom struggle. But, now it was time to build a nation from scratch. And Indians seemed ready for the challenges, of which there were many. Jawaharlal Nehru was nominated as the first Prime Minister of independent India. Primarily, there were millions of refugees who had come from Pakistan with neither homes and jobs nor any means of securing them. Next, the pockets of princely states had to be diplomatically managed because otherwise, they would create major administrative issues. Thanks to Sardar Vallabh Bhai Patel's diplomacy only three states were left to sign the instrument of accession—Jammu and Kashmir, Junagadh, and Hyderabad. But still, this was a crucial issue because of the strategic placement of these states. And lastly, a constitution had to be formed to ensure that the independence that people had fought for remained secure for ages to come.

But before Indian people could recover from the shock of

partition, they had to face yet another catastrophe. On January 30th, 1948, Gandhi was shot as he was about to conduct one of his daily multifaith prayer meetings by a man called Nathuram Godse. Godse was a member of the right-wing organizations mentioned before—the Hindu Mahasabha and the Rashtriya Swayamsevak Sangh (RSS). He was vehemently opposed to Gandhi's ideals and believed that he had always engaged in appeasement politics. He feared that if Gandhi were to live, he would divide the country even further to appease the minorities. He was arrested and was given the death sentence. Regardless of whether people agreed with Gandhi or not, losing him was yet another blow to the already wounded people.

Regardless, there was no time to stop and Nehru put his best men to work. Sardar Vallabh Bhai Patel, a seasoned diplomat, and the Deputy Prime Minister, was given the task of integrating the remaining princely states into the federation of India. Junagadh and Hyderabad had joined the Indian state by 1948.

The situation with Kashmir proved to be tricky. Maharaja Hari Singh of Kashmir had also acceded his state to India on October 26th, 1947, a little after the Indian independence. But Pakistan claimed that their armies were in standstill agreement with the king, therefore making the accession instrument null and void. During this time, Lord Mountbatten was still the Viceroy and he accepted Hari Singh's accession but also mentioned that a referendum with the people of Kashmir would be conducted. However, the referendum never happened and Kashmir is still the bone of contention between the two countries. Multiple wars have been fought between the two countries for control over this strategically placed state.

The problem of the Constitution was also resolved as Nehru put that responsibility on the able shoulders of B. R. Ambedkar. Being from a socially oppressed caste and hailing from a humble background, Ambedkar was of the opinion that the Constitution had to be a tool for social reform if nothing else. He sought to base this all-important national document on equality and freedom. India was to be the largest democracy where people would have the right to vote for their representatives and thus play an indirect role in the functioning of the state. India became a republic on January 26th, 1950.

The last of the worries was the rehabilitation of the refugees. This concern would pose the toughest challenge yet. Refugees who had lost everything obviously didn't have a positive outlook towards the government. But Nehru and his bureaucrats were laying the plan for the future. The idea was to develop new hubs of development in unutilized regions. Central Province (present-day Chattisgarh, Madhya Pradesh, Maharashtra) seemed like a good option. To hasten this process, an agricultural revolution was also undertaken and many new loan schemes were introduced to help people rebuild their lives.

CONCLUSION
THE NEW INDIA

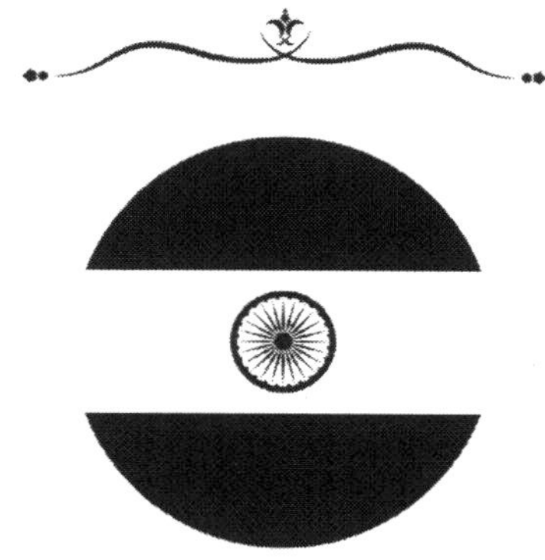

India, as a culture and as a nation, has had a colorful history. Over the centuries, it has been a melting pot of various traditions, heritages, and beliefs. Sure, it has been painful at times, and at times even bizarre, but it has survived all the storms and maybe even come out stronger. Partition is the unfortunate proof. But no one can deny that India emerged out of the ordeal successfully and has been a growing formidable economy on the world map.

But the journey since independence has not been easy. At the first elections in 1952, Nehru was re-elected as the Prime Minister, and also again in 1957 and 1962. He was a people's man after all. The developmental plans were divided into five-year plans. The first two five-year plans rightly focused on the development of agriculture and industries. This gave an impetus to rapid growth first of the rural sector and then of the urban sector. The states were also reorganized and the French and Portuguese colonies were also acquired through military offensive.

While India had positive global relations, it has had a murky history with its border neighbors. Immediately

after independence, the Kashmir war was fought in 1947–48

which concluded in Pakistan occupying a part of Kashmir, which is still called POK (Pakistan-Occupied-Kashmir). Wars and ceasefires have continued in Kashmir all along, making it difficult for people to have a normal life. Nehru is often blamed for his approach with Pakistan as well as for the defeat of Indian forces by China in 1962.

For a long time, Congress had a great hold over the political scene in the country. India saw greats like Lal Bahadur Shastri, Morarji Desai, and so on assume positions of power. However, it started becoming apparent that the Nehru/Gandhi family was not willing to let go of its iron clasp over the political happenings.

Nehru's daughter Indira Gandhi was no doubt a formidable and loved leader. But she also turned out to be one who made the most controversial decisions including declaring a state of emergency. She was eventually assassinated by her Sikh bodyguards. As years passed by these dissatisfactions became prominent and the changing face of Indian politics resulted in a lowered appreciation for the policies of Congress. Eventually, many new parties emerged and the nation has proved to be one of the most vibrant democracies in the world.

As India entered into the 21st century, the tools and styles of politics have changed but what remains steadfast is the people's hope to elect something better. Regardless of the setbacks this nation has faced every now and then, it has surely emerged victorious. During the transfer of power from the British to the Indian state, many wondered if India was ready. Many speculated that the Indian democracy would be nothing but a disaster. But the truth is Indian democracy has only matured over the years. It doesn't mean there are no problems—there certainly are. The right-wing movement that is catching on across the world has also had its impact on India but it continues to evolve through these changes.

If you enjoyed reading this book and found it helpful, please leave a review on Amazon. It shall help us reach more curious minds with this brilliant story. May we all learn from stories and histories.

REFERENCES

THE HISTORY OF CHINA

Beazley, C. R. (1903). The texts and versions of John de Plano Carpini and William de Rubruquis, as printed for the first time by Hakluyt in 1598, together with some shorter pieces (in Latin and English). London: Hakluyt Society.

Bergreen, L. (2007). Marco Polo: From Venice to Xanadu. Knopf.

Bo, Y. (1991). Complete Works. China Press.

Campbell, C. (2019). 'The Entire System Is Designed to Suppress Us.' What the Chinese Surveillance State Means for the Rest of the World. Time. URL: https://time.com/5735411/china-surveillance-privacy-issues/

Cao, D. & Sun. Y. (2011). China's History. Cengage Learning Asia Pte Ltd.

Chen, Y. J. (2018). Frontier, Fortification, and Forestation: Defensive Woodland on the Song-Liao Border in the Long Eleventh Century. Journal of Chinese History.

China Daily (2007). The Era of Prosperity is Upon Us. www.chinadaily.com.cn. URL: http://www.chinadaily.com.cn/opinion/2007-10/19/content_6243676.htm

Chinese script, Hangzhou. (2020). In www.unsplash.com. Retrieved December 9, 2021, from https://www.unsplash.com/photos/icVaVSd-8kQ

Chinese temple, Leshan. (2018). In www.pexels.com. Retrieved December 9, 2021, from https://www.pexels.com/photo/photography-of-the-temple-879359/

CIA (2021). China: The World Factbook. URL: https://www.cia.gov/the-world-factbook/countries/china/

Council on Foreign Relations. (2021). Territorial Disputes in the South China Sea. www.cfr.org. URL: https://www.cfr.org/global-conflict-tracker/conflict/territorial-disputes-south-china-sea

Dai, Y. & Gong, S. (2003). History of China: Illustrated Student Edition. Intelligence Press.

Ebrey, P. B. (2010). The Cambridge Illustrated History of China. Cambridge University Press.

Elverskog, J. (2010). Buddhism and Islam on the Silk Road. University of Pennsylvania Press.

Ferguson, J. C. & Masaharu, A. (1928). The Mythology of All Races: Volume VIII. Marshall Jones Company.

Finer, S. E. (1999) The History of Government from the Earliest Times: Volume III: Empires, Monarchies, and the Modern State. Oxford University Press.

Fowler, J. (2005). An Introduction to the Philosophy and Religion of

Taoism: Pathways to Immortality. Brighton: Sussex Academic Press.

Gascoigne, B. & Gascoigne, C. (2003). The Dynasties of China. Perseus Books Group.

Gardner, D. K. (2014). Confucianism: A Very Short Introduction. Oxford.

Gill, B. & O'Hanlon, M. E. (1999). China's Hollow Military. Brookings. URL: https://www.brookings.edu/articles/chinas-hollow-military/

Great Wall, Jinshanling. (2020). In www.unsplash.com. Retrieved December 9, 2021, from https://www.unsplash.com/photos/E13mcj-2TLE

Jisheng, W. (2012). Tombstone: The Untold Story of Mao's Great Famine. Allen Lane.

Johnson, C. A. (1963). Peasant Nationalism and Communist Power: The Emergence of Revolutionary China, 1937-1945. The Journal of Politics.

Keay, J. (2009). China: A History. Basic Books.

Kerr, G. (2013). A Short History of China: From Ancient Dynasties to Economic Powerhouse. Pocket Essentials.

Kopf, D. & Lahiri, T. (2018). The astonishing impact of China's 1978 reforms, in charts. Quartz. URL: https://qz.com/1498654/the-astonishing-impact-of-chinas-1978-reforms-in-charts/

Li, Z. (1994). The Private Life of Chairman Mao. New York: Random House.

Longmen Grottoes. (2021). In www.pexels.com. Retrieved December 9, 2021, from https://www.pexels.com/photo/buddha-statues-in-the-longmen-grottoes-8508726/

MacFarquhar, R. & Schoenhals, M. (2008). Mao's Last Revolution. Harvard University Press (2008).

Man, J. (2014). The Mongol Empire: Genghis Khan, His Heirs, and the Founding of Modern China. Bantam Press.

Mongol Falconer. (2018). In www.pexels.com. Retrieved December 9, 2021, from https://www.pexels.com/photo/cold-snow-fashion-man-6408355/

Morrison, W. M. (2019). China's Economic Rise: History, Trends, Challenges, and Implications for the United States. www.everycrsreport.com. URL: https://www.everycrsreport.com/reports/RL33534.html#_Toc12530884

Myers, S. L. (2021). The Moon, Mars, and Beyond: China's Ambitious Plans in Space. The New York Times. URL: https://www.nytimes.com/article/china-mars-space.html

Perdue, P. C. (2005). China Marches West: The Qing Conquest of Central Eurasia. Belknap Press of Harvard University.

Peterson, B. B. (2000). Notable Women of China: Shang Dynasty to the Early Twentieth Century. Routledge.

Rawski, T. G. (2008). China's Great Transformation. Cambridge University Press.

Sima, Q. translated by Watson, B. (1993). Records of the Grand Historian. Columbia University Press.

Shanghai. (2017). In www.pexels.com. Retrieved December 9, 2021, from https://www.pexels.com/photo/landscape-photo-of-night-city-745243/

Spence, J. D. (2013). The Search for Modern China. W. W. Norton & Company.

Subcommittee on International Human Rights of the Canadian House of Commons Standing Committee on Foreign Affairs and International Development (2020). Statement by the Subcommittee on International Human Rights concerning the human rights situation of Uyghurs and other Turkic Muslims in Xinjiang, China.

Summer Palace, Beijing. (2020). In www.pexels.com. Retrieved December 9, 2021, from https://www.pexels.com/photo/photo-of-a-palace-3960018/

Sussman, G. D. (2011). Was the Black Death in India and China? City University of New York Academic Works.

Szczepanski, K. (2019). Puyi, China's Last Emperor. ThoughtCo. URL: https://www.thoughtco.com/puyi-chinas-last-emperor-195612

Taagepera, R. (1997). Expansion and Contraction Patterns of Large Polities: Context for Russia. International Studies Quarterly. 41 (3): 492-502.

Talbot, M. (1991). The Holographic Universe. Harper Collins.

Temple of Heaven, Beijing. (2007). In www.pexels.com. Retrieved December 9, 2021, from https://www.pexels.com/photo/a-temple-under-the-blue-sky-5760659/

Terracotta Warriors, Xian. (2020). In www.unsplash.com. Retrieved December 9, 2021, from https://www.unsplash.com/photos/gUtcrNunbCM

Tiananmen Square, Beijing. (2020). In www.pexels.com. Retrieved December 9, 2021, from https://www.pexels.com/photo/people-walking-on-street-near-red-and-white-building-5075259/

Twitchett, D. (1998). The Cambridge History of China Volume 7 The Ming Dynasty 1368-1644, Part I. Cambridge University Press.

Upton-McLauchlin, S. (2013). A Guide to Hanyu Pinyin and Correct Chinese Pronunciation. The China Culture Corner. URL: https://chinaculturecorner.com/2013/09/22/pronouncing-chinese-pinyin/

Wilson Center. China's Soft Power Campaign. www.wilsoncenter.org. URL: https://www.wilsoncenter.org/chinas-soft-power-campaign/

Wright, D. C. (2011). The History of China. Greenwood.

Wu et al (2016). Outburst flood at 1920 BCE supports historicity of China's Great Flood and the Xia dynasty. Science. 353 (6299).

Zhang, Q. (2015). An Introduction to Chinese History and Culture. Springer.

Zhao et al (2015). Ancient DNA Reveals That the Genetic Structure of the Northern Han Chinese Was Shaped Prior to three-thousand Years Ago. PLoS ONE.

Zhao, S. (1993). Deng Xiapoing's Southern Tour: Elite Politics in Post-Tiananmen China. Asian Survey. 33 (8) 739-756.

JAPANESE HISTORY

Akatani, M. (2016). [The Cause of Death of Taira no Kiyomori: A Possible Connection with the Death of Fujiwara no Kunitsuna]. *Nihon Ishigaku Zasshi. [Journal of Japanese History of Medicine]*, *62*(1), 3–15. https://pubmed.ncbi.nlm.nih.gov/27464420/.

All Types of Japanese Swords (history and how they were used). (2020, August 29). Www.youtube.com. https://www.youtube.com/watch?v=0T8m3AOV_IY.

Axelrod, J. (2019). *NPR Choice page*. Npr.org. https://www.npr.org/sections/codeswitch/2019/08/11/742293305/a-century-later-the-treaty-of-versailles-and-its-rejection-of-racial-equality.

Commodore Perry and the Opening of Japan. (2021, February 7). Www.youtube.com. https://www.youtube.com/watch?v=MaZ95O6RmAc.

Emperor Go-Daigo. (2020, June 9). Wikipedia. https://en.wikipedia.org/wiki/Emperor_Go-Daigo.

Feature History. (2017). Feature History - Meiji Restoration. On YouTube. https://www.youtube.com/watch?v=Y_b58Rpg2YY.

History Summarized: The Meiji Restoration. (2020, May 8). Www.youtube.com. https://www.youtube.com/watch?v=Y5zlKYYp7bs.

How'd It Happen? History. (2017). What Happened to Japan after WW2? (How'd It Happen? History). In *YouTube*. https://www.youtube.com/watch?v=Lg4tQOEqU30.

https://www.facebook.com/thoughtcodotcom. (2019). *How to Be Beautiful in Heian Era Japan*. ThoughtCo. https://www.thoughtco.com/beauty-in-heian-japan-195557.

Imperial Regalia of Japan. (2020, April 26). Wikipedia. https://en.wikipedia.org/wiki/Imperial_Regalia_of_Japan.

Izanagi. (2020, November 8). Wikipedia. https://en.wikipedia.org/wiki/Izanagi

Japan Omnibus - History - Early Japanese History. (2018). Japan-Zone.com. https://www.japan-zone.com/omnibus/history1.shtml.

Japanese history: Postwar. (2002, June 9). Japan-Guide.com. https://www.japan-guide.com/e/e2124.html.

Japanese Mythology - Myth Encyclopedia - god, story, legend, names, ancient, tree, famous, animal, world, Chinese. (2010).

Mythencyclopedia.com. http://www.mythencyclopedia.com/Iz-Le/Japanese-Mythology.html.

Kiger, P. J. (2019, September 20). *10 Inventions From China's Han Dynasty That Changed the World.* HISTORY. https://www.history.com/news/han-dynasty-inventions.

Life in Edo Japan (1603-1868). (2019, April 27). Www.youtube.com. https://www.youtube.com/watch?v=wIygLo_W1Sw&t=456s.

Linfamy. (2019). Life of Early Japanese Women (So Much Cheating...) | History of Japan 38 [YouTube Video]. In *YouTube*. https://www.youtube.com/watch?v=Ylom3pm5SCo.

Minamoto no Yoritomo. (2020, March 11). Wikipedia. https://en.wikipedia.org/wiki/Minamoto_no_Yoritomo.

Mongol invasions of Japan. (2020, June 4). Wikipedia. https://en.wikipedia.org/wiki/Mongol_invasions_of_Japan.

Morison, S. E. (1967). Old Bruin Commodore Matthew C .perry 1794-1858. In *Internet Archive*. https://archive.org/stream/in.ernet.dli.2015.130945/2015.130945.Old-Bruin-Commodore-Methew-C-perry-1794-1858_djvu.txt.

Origins of the Yayoi people. (2008, June 27). Heritage of Japan. https://heritageofjapan.wordpress.com/yayoi-era-yields-up-rice/who-were-the-yayoi-people/.

Prehistory of Japan (Paleolithic, Jōmon and Yayoi periods). (n.d.). Www.youtube.com. Retrieved November 30, 2021, from https://www.youtube.com/watch?v=8Q4fRT081-0.

Proctor, M. (2015, June 25). *Japanese Mythology: 5 Ancient Myths and Legends.* TakeLessons Blog. https://takelessons.com/blog/japanese-mythology-z05.

Taika era reforms | Japanese history | Britannica. (2019). In *Encyclopædia Britannica*. https://www.britannica.com/event/Taika-era-reforms.

The Heian Period, an Age of Art...Ending in a Shogunate | History of Japan 34. (n.d.). Www.youtube.com. Retrieved December 2, 2021, from https://www.youtube.com/watch?v=9z8ZZezVmfw.

The Jomon, a 10,000 Year Old Culture (and Pots!) | History of Japan 3. (n.d.). Www.youtube.com. Retrieved November 30, 2021, from https://www.youtube.com/watch?v=gDBB5nazfM4.

The Rise of Japan: How did Japan become one of the World's Largest Economies? (2021, January 31). Www.youtube.com. https://www.youtube.com/watch?v=ytrpRLOaPzM

The Shogunate. (2019). The Samurai Tradition of Taking Heads. On *YouTube*. https://www.youtube.com/watch?v=TXPrkZ5Kpmo.

The Yayoi Arrive...and Change EVERYTHING! | History of Japan 4. (n.d.). Www.youtube.com. https://www.youtube.com/watch?v=bDnV9UvrpaU&t=5s.

Truman Statement on Hiroshima. (n.d.). Atomic Heritage Foundation.

https://www.atomicheritage.org/key-documents/truman-statement-hiroshima#:~:text=If%20they%20do%20not%20now.

Volcanoes of Japan: facts & information / VolcanoDiscovery. (2020). Volcanodiscovery.com. https://www.volcanodiscovery.com/japan.html.

W, S. (2013, November 8). *The Ainu*. Tofugu. https://www.tofugu.com/japan/ainu-japan/

Warring States Japan: Sengoku Jidai - Battle of Okehazama - Extra History - #1. (2014, November 8). Www.youtube.com. https://www.youtube.com/watch?v=hDsdkoln59A&list=PLhyKYa0YJ_5A649vEQk37316BH8FsaU24.

Warring States Japan: Sengoku Jidai - How Toyotomi Unified Japan - Extra History - #5. (2015, January 17). Www.youtube.com. https://www.youtube.com/watch?v=lBD8OAegEwo&list=PLhyKYa0YJ_5A649vEQk37316BH8FsaU24&index=5.

Warring States Japan: Sengoku Jidai - The Campaign of Sekigahara - Extra History - #6. (2015, January 31). Www.youtube.com. https://www.youtube.com/watch?v=5vscOHPFUfo&list=PLhyKYa0YJ_5A649vEQk37316BH8FsaU24&index=6.

Warring States Japan: Sengoku Jidai - The Death of Oda Nobunaga - Extra History - #4. (2014, December 20). Www.youtube.com. https://www.youtube.com/watch?v=ht6h4-MsMOY&list=PLhyKYa0YJ_5A649vEQk37316BH8FsaU24&index=4.

Warring States Japan: Sengoku Jidai - The Siege of Inabayama Castle - Extra History - #2. (2014, November 22). Www.youtube.com. https://www.youtube.com/watch?v=I2yT2nitGDk&list=PLhyKYa0YJ_5A649vEQk37316BH8FsaU24&index=2.

Warring States Japan: Sengoku Jidai - Warrior Monks of Hongan-ji and Hiei - Extra History - #3. (2014, December 6). Www.youtube.com. https://www.youtube.com/watch?v=G3frtoMaxZE&list=PLhyKYa0YJ_5A649vEQk37316BH8FsaU24&index=3.

Why Japan Got off Easy in WW2 - The HORRIBLE Atrocities of the Japanese Empire. (2021, June 6). Www.youtube.com. http://youtube.com/watch?v=uBEmMeZOYaI.

Wikipedia Contributors. (2019a, March 12). *Genpei War*. Wikipedia; Wikimedia Foundation. https://en.wikipedia.org/wiki/Genpei_War.

Wikipedia Contributors. (2019b, July 3). *Nara period*. Wikipedia; Wikimedia Foundation. https://en.wikipedia.org/wiki/Nara_period.

Wikipedia Contributors. (2019c, September 14). *Sengoku period*. Wikipedia; Wikimedia Foundation. https://en.wikipedia.org/wiki/Sengoku_period.

Wikipedia Contributors. (2021a, April 18). *Ōnin War*. Wikipedia; Wikimedia Foundation. https://en.wikipedia.org/wiki/%C5%8Cnin_War.

Wikipedia Contributors. (2021b, August 12). *Dōkyō*. Wikipedia; Wikimedia Foundation. https://en.wikipedia.org/wiki/D%C5%8Dky%C5%8D.

Wikipedia Contributors. (2021c, October 27). *Jōkyū War*. Wikipedia; Wikimedia Foundation. https://en.wikipedia.org/wiki/J%C5%8Dky%C5%AB_War.

WorldAtlas. (2019, January 18). *Why Is Volcanic Soil Fertile?* WorldAtlas. https://www.worldatlas.com/articles/why-is-volcanic-soil-fertile.html.

THE HISTORY OF INDIA

Byju's. (2021, August 2). *How the Kalinga war changed Emperor Ashoka | Class 6 | Learn with Byju's*. YouTube. https://www.youtube.com/watch?v=b3oKeI8zzeQ

Chandra, B., Mukherjee, M., Mukherjee, A., Mahajan, S., & Panikkar, K. N. (2003). *India's struggle for independence, 1857-1947*. Penguin.

Dabas, M. (2017, August 17). *Trending stories on Indian lifestyle, culture, relationships, food, travel, entertainment, news & new technology news*. Indiatimes. https://www.indiatimes.com/news/india/here-s-how-radcliff-line-was-drawn-on-this-day-and-lahore-could-not-become-a-part-of-india-328012.html

Dalrymple, W. (2015, June 22). *The mutual genocide of Indian Partition*. The New Yorker. https://www.newyorker.com/magazine/2015/06/29/the-great-divide-books-dalrymple

History's Histories. (2018). *India Gupta empire*. http://www.historyshistories.com/india-gupta-empire.html

Kapoor, R. (2021, August 14). *Build the refugee, build the state: Development & rehabilitation in post-partition india*. Refugee History. http://refugeehistory.org/blog/2017/8/12/build-the-refugee-build-the-state-development-rehabilitation-in-post-partition-india

Keay, J. (2011). *India: A history*. Crane Library At The University Of British Columbia.

Majumdar, R. C., Raychaudhuri, H. C., & Datta, K. (1974). *An advanced history of India*. Delhi.

Mark, J. (2020, May 24). *Ashoka the Great*. World History Encyclopedia. https://www.worldhistory.org/Ashoka_the_Great/

National Geographic Society. (2020, August 20). *Mauryan empire.* National Geographic Society. https://www.nationalgeographic.org/encyclopedia/mauryan-empire/#:~:text=The%20Mauryan%20Empire%2C%20which%20formed

Pal, S. (2017, December 16). *The making of a nation: How Sardar Patel integrated 562 princely states.* The Better India. https://www.thebetterindia.com/124500/sardar-patel-vp-menon-integration-princely-states-india-independence/

Paul, S. (2021, March 17). *Yes, Gandhi did his utmost to save the lives of Bhagat Singh, Sukhdev and Rajguru, writes Sumit Paul.* Free Press Journal. https://www.freepressjournal.in/analysis/yes-gandhi-did-his-utmost-to-save-the-lives-of-bhagat-singh-sukhdev-and-rajguru-writes-sumit-paul

Pletcher, K. (2021, February 26). *Gandhi-Irwin Pact | Indian history.* Encyclopedia Britannica. https://www.britannica.com/event/Gandhi-Irwin-Pact

Rathee, D. (2021, August 15). *Partition 1947 / Why it happened? | India and Pakistan | Dhruv Rathee.* YouTube. https://www.youtube.com/watch?v=r2kKsjZPrVI

Study IQ Education. (2019, October 6). *Biography of Muhammad Ali Jinnah, Founder and first governor general of Pakistan.* YouTube. https://www.youtube.com/watch?v=NOKcSYZZwpg

Thapar, R. (2015). *The Penguin history of early India: from the origins to A.D.1300.* Penguin Books.

Yadav, A. K., & Chaudhary, S. (2021, April 14). *BR Ambedkar: Father of our Constitution and radical social thinker.* TheLeaflet. https://www.theleaflet.in/br-ambedkar-father-of-our-constitution-and-radical-social-thinker/

FREE BONUS FROM HBA: EBOOK BUNDLE

Greetings!

First of all, thank you for reading our books. As fellow passionate readers of History and Mythology, we aim to create the very best books for our readers.

Now, we invite you to join our VIP list. As a welcome gift, we offer the History & Mythology Ebook Bundle below for free. Plus you can be the first to receive new books and exclusives! Remember it's 100% free to join.

Simply scan the QR code down below to join.

OTHER BOOKS BY HISTORY BROUGHT ALIVE

Available now in Ebook, Paperback, Hardcover, and Audiobook in all regions.

Other books:

For Kids:

HISTORY & MYTHOLOGY FOR KIDS
HISTORY BROUGHT ALIVE

GREEK MYTHOLOGY FOR KIDS
HISTORY BROUGHT ALIVE

EGYPTIAN MYTHOLOGY FOR KIDS
HISTORY BROUGHT ALIVE

MYTHOLOGY FOR KIDS
HISTORY BROUGHT ALIVE

THE HISTORY OF ENGLAND FOR KIDS
HISTORY BROUGHT ALIVE

NATIVE AMERICAN HISTORY FOR KIDS
Explore Timeless Tales, Myths, Legends, Bedtime Stories & Much More from The Native Indigenous Americans
HISTORY BROUGHT ALIVE

CELTIC HISTORY & MYTHOLOGY FOR KIDS
Explore Timeless Tales, Characters, History, & Legendary Stories from The Celts
HISTORY BROUGHT ALIVE

WORLD WAR 2 HISTORY FOR KIDS
A Timeline of Fascinating Facts, Characters and Stories of Courage that Inspire & Educate
HISTORY BROUGHT ALIVE

WORLD WAR 1 HISTORY FOR KIDS
HISTORY BROUGHT ALIVE

HISTORY OF ASIA

We sincerely hope you enjoyed our new book ***"History of Asia"***. We would greatly appreciate your feedback with an honest review at the place of purchase.

First and foremost, we are always looking to grow and improve as a team. It is reassuring to hear what works, as well as receive constructive feedback on what should improve. Second, starting out as an unknown author is exceedingly difficult, and Amazon reviews go a long way toward making the journey out of anonymity possible. Please take a few minutes to write an honest review.

Best regards,

History Brought Alive

http://historybroughtalive.com/

Made in the USA
Columbia, SC
03 April 2024

4efe05bf-bb05-4f7d-b083-50397589f795R01